Weathering the Storm

The Port of Liverpool Building, home of the Mersey Docks and Harbour Board, and Company, 1907–1993

The new offices of the Mersey Docks and Harbour Company, opened in 1993

Weathering the Storm

THE MERSEY DOCKS FINANCIAL CRISIS 1970–74

Anthony Lynch

LIVERPOOL UNIVERSITY PRESS

First published 1994 by
LIVERPOOL UNIVERSITY PRESS
PO Box 147
Liverpool
L69 3BX

British Library Cataloguing-in-Publication Data
A British Library CIP Record is available
ISBN 0 85323 419 1 (cased)
ISBN 0 85323 429 9 (paper)

Set in Linotron 202 Garamond by
Wilmaset Limited, Birkenhead, Wirral

Printed and bound in the European Union by
Bell and Bain Limited, Glasgow

CONTENTS

ACKNOWLEDGEMENTS

The following quoted extracts from *The Times* are copyright Times Newspapers Limited and are reprinted by permission. They may not be copied.

pp. 42–43: 'Government offer £10–£20m loan to Mersey docks board' by Michael Baily, 14 November 1970.

p. 43: 'Hopes of state help fade for Mersey Board' by Michael Baily, 21 November 1970.

pp. 52–53: 'The Mersey Docks' by Ian Morison, 4 December 1970.

pp. 97-99: 'A Savage Write-Down', 31 May 1973.

pp. 121–22: 'Time for decisions by Mersey bondholders' by The Financial Editor, 28 May 1974.

FOREWORD

The winter of 1970–71 was probably the Port of Liverpool's darkest hour, at least in peace time. The container revolution (the technological change in the method of the carriage of goods by sea from break-bulk to transportation in containers) was having a major impact on the size and design of ships, the layout of port facilities and the patterns of sea trade. The Liverpool docks were built mainly in the nineteenth century for the general cargo ships of that time and though they had undergone a continuous process of adaptation and modernisation the systems still consisted essentially of a line of finger docks with narrow quays backed by transit sheds designed for the temporary storage of relatively small consignments of general cargo. They were quite unsuitable for containers.

Moreover, the constitution of the Mersey Docks and Harbour Board and its capital structure were still based largely on the concepts embodied in Acts of Parliament of 1857–58 by which the Board was set up. These were likewise unsuitable to deal with the rapidly changing situation of the last three decades of the twentieth century. The port industry's industrial relations structures were also ill-equipped to adjust to the new technology.

The Board had started to tackle the physical constraints by the construction of the new container and bulk-cargo facilities at Seaforth, the largest and most costly development in the Port's history, but during the years of this construction the Board's fortunes fell into a trough.

The 1971 Act, which transformed the Board into the Company and prescribed the framework for the modernisation of its capital structure, was at the time highly controversial. Events moved so fast as to blur the wider view. Now that over 20 years have passed it is appropriate to try to give a balanced account of the events of 1970 to 1974.

Views may still differ as to the rightness of the steps taken to resolve the crisis. It cannot be denied that many people and financial institutions suffered loss when the loans they had made to the Board were written down. However, it is surely now clear that the resultant constitution and capital structure are far better suited to the business environment of today than what they replaced. As Tony Lynch describes, the turnround was slow and painful. His epilogue stops at 1989 when the Company's capital reconstruction could be said to have achieved the Company's rehabilitation in the City, confirmed by the rights share issue of 1993. That the Company continues to go from strength to strength is illustrated by the fact that today it is listed by the *Financial Times* among Britain's top 500 companies. In 1993 it made a profit before taxation of £20,865,000 on a turnover of £98,420,000. The Port of Liverpool, a dynamic and expanding operation, remains at the core of the Company activities; the 2,000 acres of docks on both banks of the River Mersey, at Liverpool and Birkenhead, handled 29,300,000 tonnes of cargo in 1993, three times the volume handled just 10 years before. Liverpool is the United Kingdom's leading port for trade with the Eastern Seaboard of North America; for trade with Ireland; for imports of grain; for exports of scrap metal; and the Port handles large volumes of other cargoes including timber and forest products, edible oils and fats, crude oil, fossil fuel and traditional general cargo.

In October, 1993, the Company acquired Medway Ports Limited in Kent, including a 22 mile stretch of the river from its mouth and the significant South East ports of Sheerness and Chatham. The £104 million acquisition established the Company as the UK's second largest port group and added to its portfolio of trading interests complementary areas of cargo such as the import and export of cars and the movement of fresh fruit, for both of which Sheerness is the country's major port. The acquisition of strategically placed ports in the South East of England also combines with the Port of Liverpool's location on the West Coast and at the centre of Great Britain, to create a shipping and distribution network encompassing the country's major areas of production and population.

It is right to acknowledge the debt which the Company owes to those who steered it through this most critical period of its history, laying the foundations for its present prosperity, among them Mr. Bob Edwards, Sir John Cuckney and Sir John Page, others mentioned in this book, and many not mentioned.

TREVOR FURLONG
Managing Director and Chief Executive
Mersey Docks and Harbour Company

PREFACE

It is now over 20 years since the Mersey Docks and Harbour Board was transformed into the Mersey Docks and Harbour Company, but old habits die hard and many people still think and speak of 'the Board'. Even the B.B.C. as recently as 1993 referred in a North West Regional news item to the *Board*'s Birkenhead docks.

However, the passing of the Mersey Docks and Harbour Act 1971 marked more than a merely legalistic change. The Port of Liverpool was as near to terminal closure in the winter of 1970 as at any time in its 250–year history. The 1971 Act can be seen as a turning point and, though the Company was effectively on a life support machine for many years thereafter, it emerged in the 1980s as a thriving and self-confident business.

This is not a general history of Mersey Docks, even in respect of the period 1970–74 with which it is mainly concerned. It deals only with the financial crisis and its resolution, and that largely from a political and legal viewpoint. Such important topics as the construction of the Royal Seaforth Dock, the largest dock development in the Port's history, or the turbulent industrial relations events of the period are touched on only insofar as they impinged on the financial crisis. No doubt in time a general history of the Port will be written to continue on from 1963 when A. S. Mountfield's *Western Gateway* left off.

I have also avoided making any explicit evaluation of the several contributory causes of the crisis or the appropriateness of the steps taken to resolve it.

My objective has been to try to compile a record of the events of 1970–74 while the memory of some of those principally involved is still reasonably fresh. I am accordingly indebted to Sir John Cuckney and Sir John Page, successive chairmen of the Board/Company, Mr. R. S. F. Edwards, Director General of the Board and the late Mr. Hugh Wrigglesworth, Finance Director of the Company, for their comments on my draft. I am grateful also to Mr. A. P. Nute, a former

Assistant Secretary of the Company and an expert on the Port's history, both for commenting on my draft and for help in producing this book. Mr. Adrian Jarvis, Curator, Port History at the Merseyside Maritime Museum, has given both advice and encouragement.

I acknowledge considerable support in the preparation and publication of this book from the Company, in the persons especially of Mr. Trevor Furlong, Managing Director and Chief Executive, and Mr. W. Bowley, Director of Legal Services.

At a practical level my greatest debt of gratitude is to Mr. Paul Eaton, Assistant Secretary, who has been most assiduous in locating the many papers and documents which I have used in my research, and to Mrs. S. McNicholl who has grappled with my handwritten script to turn it into a beautifully presented typescript fit to be shown to those whom I asked to comment and presented to the printers. I am especially grateful for their help as they had to fit it into their normal work and, moreover, at a time when the Company was moving out of the Dock Office and into the new Maritime Centre at Seaforth. The work of researching the records was facilitated by the meticulous filing system operated by my former secretary, Miss Audrey Smith (Mrs. Herd).

I must add the usual disclaimer. Whilst acknowledging the help of those mentioned above, I accept full responsibility for the final result. Anybody who was swept up in the crisis as I was, as last Secretary of the Board and first Secretary of the Company, could not be dispassionate about what happened. I have tried to give an objective account of those events but have no illusions that I have wholly succeeded. Maybe I or some successor may revise it when the Government records for the period become available after the turn of the century.

Note on terminology: I have set out to follow the usage of 'the Board is/was' when referring to the corporate entity, and 'the board are/were' when referring to the body of men (it was always men) sitting round a board-room table. The distinction is not always clear-cut and diligent readers may well find lapses. (Of course, when quoting I have retained the usage of the original which does not always correspond to the above).

Chapter 1
THE PUBLIC TRUST

The first dock in Liverpool was constructed under the authority of an Act of Parliament of 1709, promoted by the Corporation of Liverpool, by developing the mouth of the Pool, a natural inlet from the Mersey. This dock, the Old Dock as it came to be known, was completed in 1715, and it and the series of docks subsequently constructed to the north and south of the Old Dock were administered by the Corporation of Liverpool. During the 18th Century the Corporation acted directly through a Committee of its own members, but in 1811 the Corporation was established as a statutory body called 'The Trustees of the Liverpool Docks' to manage the dock estate and the port, their powers being formally delegated to a Committee of 21 members of the Corporation. In 1825 the constitution of this Committee was changed to include in its 21 members eight to be elected from time to time by Liverpool-based merchants, shipowners and agents who had paid prescribed amounts by way of dock charges, the other members including the Chairman continuing to be members of the Common Council. Under an Act of 1825 which effected this change in the Committee's constitution, a two-thirds majority of members of the Common Council present was necessary to override any decision of the Committee, instead of a bare majority as previously.

The constitution of the Committee was again altered by an Act of 1851. Henceforth the Committee was to consist of 12 Common Council members and 12 dock rate payers, the Chairman to be elected from among the councillors; the Corporation retained its power to override the Committee.

In the 1840s and 1850s various attempts were made to start the development of a rival dock system on the Birkenhead side of the River Mersey, based principally on the exploitation of the Wallasey Pool, a natural inlet and the counterpart of the Pool of Liverpool from which Liverpool's docks had originated.

In 1855, four private Bills were promoted in Parliament to authorise works in Birkenhead and to relieve trade using the Birkenhead Docks from payment of Town Dues, together with two private Bills relating to the Liverpool Docks. These Bills were all referred to one Committee of the House of Commons who suggested that it would be to the general public advantage for the docks on both sides of the River Mersey to be administered as one system. In accordance with this suggestion, the Corporation of Liverpool agreed to purchase the undertakings of the Birkenhead Dock Trustees and the Birkenhead Dock Company, this agreement being confirmed by the Birkenhead Docks Act 1855. However, in the Bill which the Liverpool Corporation promoted in the next session of Parliament, no provision was made for meeting the House of Commons Committee's Special Report's other suggestions, designed to guard against Liverpool's exploitation of their control of the amalgamated dock systems to the detriment of commerce.

A particular concern of the dock users over many years had been the Corporation's use of the Town Dues and Anchorage Dues charged on goods and ships entering and leaving the Port. The origin of these dues is obscure, but they can be traced back at least as far as the reign of Henry III. They were distinct from the statutory charges on ships for the upkeep of the conservancy of the river and its approaches, and on ships and goods for the provision and maintenance of the docks. One reason why port users generally resented these Town Dues was that the freemen of Liverpool were exempt from payment and consequently enjoyed an advantage over their commercial competitors. This anomaly was curtailed by the Municipal Corporations Act 1835, whereafter only those who had enjoyed the privilege before the passing of the Act continued to do so. However, the other contentious aspect of the Town Dues remained, namely that there was no obligation on the Corporation to use the revenue derived from them for the benefit of the Port, and it was alleged that they were in fact used for general municipal purposes.[1] This resentment was felt particularly, of course, by merchants from outside Liverpool who were becoming increasingly reliant on the Port for their business.

Dissatisfaction over the issue of the Town Dues and with the Corporation's failure to tackle the matters raised by the House of Commons Committee's Special Report induced the Manchester Chamber of Commerce, the Manchester Commercial Association and the Great Western Railway Company (who had a particular interest in the development of the Birkenhead Dock System) to promote a private Bill to establish a new body wholly independent of the Corporation of Liverpool to take over the Port (including the right to levy the Town and Anchorage Dues) and to manage it for the benefit of commerce generally. Despite opposition from the Corporation and the Dock Trustees, who were separately represented by Counsel before the Parliamentary Committee which considered the Bill, it was duly passed as the Mersey Docks and Harbour Act 1857 with the title 'An Act for consolidating the Docks at Liverpool and Birkenhead into One Estate and for vesting the Control and Management of them in One Public Trust'.

Thus was established, on the 1st January 1858, The Mersey Docks and Harbour Board, an autonomous corporation, designated a public trust, governed by a body whose members were predominantly its customers. The board—the governing body—was to consist of 28 members, 12 elected by those who paid dues on ships using the port, 12 elected by those who paid dues on goods and four nominated by the Conservancy Commissioners of the River Mersey. (These Commissioners were the First Lord of the Admiralty, the President of the Board of Trade and the Chancellor of the Duchy of Lancaster who had been invested by an Act of 1842[2] with limited powers to control the construction of works in the river; their powers passed to the Ministry of Transport in 1919.[3])

Though the Board's constitution has a superficial appearance of being quite democratic (to the extent that the Port's customers can be termed the 'demos'), in practice the Board became effectively a self-perpetuating oligarchy. Members were put up by various trade associations such as the powerful Liverpool Steam Ship Owners Association and the less influential Liverpool Shipowners Association (representing the owners of smaller ships), who between them shared out the 12 shipowner places. These arrangements have rarely been challenged in recent years, the last occasion being in June 1970 when a postal election under the Mersey Docks and Harbour Board Revision Order 1965[4] resulted in the victory of the Board's nominee by a ratio of 4:1.

The oligarchy was to a slight extent moderated by the Minister of Transport's nomination of four members. It had been the practice since 1930 to use this right to nominate two members who could speak for the interests of workers in the Port.

The riparian local authorities made several approaches to gain membership, as for example in 1907 when the Liverpool Corporation made a formal request to the Board to include in its next Parliamentary Bill a provision giving the Corporation the right to nominate one or more members of the Board; the Board declined to do so. Again, in practice, this was to some extent moderated by the Minister of Transport's nominations. For example, Sir Joseph Cleary was nominated in 1950 when he was Lord Mayor of Liverpool[5] and served until 1970 when, as Vice Chairman, he effectively led the Board in the critical weeks of late 1970 when Mr. Taylor the Chairman was incapacitated by illness.

The Board inherited a dock system in 1858 extending from the nearly completed Canada Dock to Brunswick Dock in Liverpool (stretching some four miles along the East shore of the river), together with the partially completed Herculaneum dock estate belonging to the Birkenhead Dock Company and two small docks and extensive partially completed works in Birkenhead.

The Mersey Docks and Harbour Act 1857 put upon the Board an obligation to promote a Bill in the next session of Parliament to consolidate the various Acts then in force and to confer any new powers necessary to carry into effect the purposes of the 1857 Act. This led to the passing of the Mersey Dock Acts Consolidation Act 1858, a statute of 368 sections and 10 schedules, much of which still remains in force.

This, in summary, is the historical origin of the Mersey Docks and Harbour Board which is more fully described in, for example, *Western Gateway* by Stuart Mountfield, a former General Manager and Secretary of the Board.[6] It is, however, in the context of this study necessary to describe more fully aspects of the Board's finances.

When the Board was established, it was required by the 1857 Act to compensate the Corporation of Liverpool for their loss of the Town and Anchorage Dues to the sum of £1.5 million and to pay them also £1,465,000 for their interest in the Birkenhead dock estate. These amounts, together with interest, were paid off over seven years. The Board also assumed responsibility for the bond debt amounting to £6,134,000. The total consideration paid by the Board was thus some £9 million, equivalent to about 17 times the purchase of the then annual revenue of £530,000 (of which the Town Dues amounted to about £130,000).

The system of financing capital expenditure by means of short-term bonds secured on the rates and dues which the Board inherited was continued as the only means of finance for the rest of the century (though it is of interest to note that in their Act of 1813 the Corporation had included an authorisation for the Treasury to direct His Majesty's Customs to lend the Trustees up to £60,000, a provision that was repealed in 1858).

To facilitate the continued expansion of the dock system, the Board promoted a private Act in 1859 to increase its borrowing powers and at the same time to establish a sinking fund to amortise its debt. It was authorised to transfer revenue surpluses to this fund up to a maximum of £100,000 per annum, which was equivalent to about a sixtieth part of its then capital debt.

As early as 1879 the Liverpool Chamber of Commerce was urging the Board to fund its debt on a longer-term basis than its short-term bonds. In 1887 the Board promoted a Bill to authorise such funding but withdrew it when the Chairman of the Committee of the House of Lords (to whom the Bill was referred) insisted, as a condition of granting the powers, on the setting up of a new form of sinking fund obliging the Board to set aside a definite sum each year, instead of the permissive power enjoyed under the 1859 Act.

The board debated the basis of the Board's financing on several occasions over the ensuing years, but no change was made until 1898 when, in spite of the opposition of the Chairman of the Finance Committee, Mr. Robert Gladstone, who argued that any Parliamentary procedure to alter the existing arrangements might open the door for stockholder representation on the board being imposed, they decided to promote a private Bill. This, which was enacted as The Mersey Docks (Finance) Act 1899, gave power to create and issue redeemable stock in such amounts, at such prices and times and on such terms and conditions as it thought fit. The Bill had contained no sinking fund proposals and on this occasion none was sought to be imposed. A schedule to the Act shows that the Board's bond debt was then just over £15.5 million and there were annuities[7] with a face value of just over £2.5 million outstanding. The first Mersey Docks and Harbour Board debenture stock was created in pursuance of these new powers in 1900, £5 million of 1930/60 stock at 3% interest. It was in effect a tap stock but proved to be a failure; only £92,000 was issued, the current political conditions, notably the South African war, being blamed.

Five years later in 1905, the Board made a further issue of £3.5 million of 3½% stock at 96.5 redeemable at par in 1935/1965, partly for the conversion of bonds and partly for public application. This issue was successful and the Board adopted the practice of creating blocks of stock to offer conversion terms to holders of bonds maturing quarter by quarter. However, after almost five years the response became disappointing and though the Board would have liked to issue further stock to fund its increasing commitments for capital expenditure, its financial advisers recommended reliance on borrowing by means of bonds in the prevailing circumstances. At this time the proportion of long-term to short-term debt was 1:3.

To alleviate unemployment after the First World War, the Government introduced an unemployment grant scheme under which 50% of the interest on monies borrowed for approved capital schemes was paid by the Government for 15 years. The Board took advantage of this scheme to complete the Gladstone Dock, whose construction had been interrupted by the War, and the construction of the Alfred 80 feet entrance to the Birkenhead docks.

In the depression of the 1930s interest rates fell and the Board revived its 3½% 1935/65 stock issued at 96.5 as a tap stock to convert bonds falling due in July 1933 and subsequent quarters. Two further issues of tap stock were created in 1934 at rates of 3¼% and 3½% redeemable 1975/85, totalling some £6 million. In 1935 they offered conversion of £9,800,000 of 3½% 1935/65 into 3¼% 1970/80 stock. This refunding operation was a success, the amount not taken up by way of conversion being covered by new applications. By now the relative proportion of long-term to short-term debt was 3:2, fixed at favourable rates of interest for lengthy periods.

During the whole of this period the Board's debt amortisation policy had continued to be governed by the 1859 Act. By 1935 the total capital expenditure paid for from borrowing was £45 million and the outstanding debt £41.5 million. The accumulated sum in the sinking fund was £6.75 million, which had been used either to repay debt or to finance capital expenditure in lieu of further borrowing.

Dock structures are, of course, built to last and with its ability to borrow as and when necessary to finance major new developments and to reborrow to extend its debt, there were those who regarded this as a satisfactory financial situation for a non-profit making port authority.

Others felt that the Board's finances needed to be put on a sounder basis, taking account of the ageing of many of the dock facilities. After consultations with the Ministry of Transport, the Mersey Docks and Harbour Board Act 1936 was passed, providing for the setting up of a new sinking fund into which annual instalments, together with interest on the accumulated balances, would be paid from revenue calculated to amortise the then total capital expenditure (less the sum of the old sinking fund) over a maximum of 90 years. The total capital expenditure to date was treated as one division in the new sinking fund regardless of the age of the various assets. Each subsequent year's capital expenditure was to be treated as a separate division of the fund. As it worked out, the first year's payment into the new fund was only £85,822, some £15,000 less than would have been paid under the 1859 Act. However, with accumulating interest the sums credited grew, as illustrated by the figures shown in Table 1, for the years immediately following the Second World War.

Table 1 *Revenue and sinking fund contributions, 1946–1953*

Year ended 1st July	Revenue surplus (deficiency)*	Sinking fund contributions
	£'000s	£'000s
1946	(671)	110
1947	519	123
1948	645	129
1949	237	135
1950	689	144
1951	293	151
1952	886	159
1953	581	168

* after charging interest.

Nevertheless, the new sinking fund was still unsatisfactory. The 90-year period took no account of the actual potential life of the assets (whether physical or commercial), especially those which were already old in 1936. In 1954 the Board's Principal Accountant recommended an acceleration of the sinking fund to have regard to a realistic estimate of the life of the assets covered. This would have raised the contribution for 1954 from £177,000 to £427,000, but the

Principal Accountant advised that this should not overstrain the Board's revenues given a reasonably good and stable level of trade and could be achieved without an increase in the rates and dues in the foreseeable future. However, the Board's Finance Committee felt that the increase was too drastic and referred the matter back for further consideration. A further report was submitted in February 1955, retaining the principle of assessing contributions by reference to weighted average estimated lives rather than the 90-year period, but calling only for an immediate increase to £320,000. This proposal was accepted by the board in June 1955.[8]

The Second World War caused major distortion of the Board's finances. In the air raids of 1940 and 1941 nearly 50 berths were put out of commission—one third of the Port—and of the remainder about one half were damaged to a greater or lesser extent. Meanwhile the Port, along with the Clyde, was under the greatest pressure to take extra ships and cargo diverted from the even more vulnerable South and East coast ports. Direct costs of the war were:

Civil defence—£1 million (75% paid by the Government)
Temporary repairs—£2 million
Restoration of War Damage—£11 million

The level of rates and dues was strictly controlled by the Government and, despite a permitted war-time surcharge from 1941 of 60% reduced to 25% in 1944, the Board ended the war with a deficit of £774,000. In 1945 it applied for and, after 3 months' delay, was granted permission to increase the surcharge from 25% (to which it had prematurely been allowed to fall just as the extra trade began to return to the South and East coast ports) to 75%. It took until 1948 for agreement to be reached with the Government on payment of almost £11 million compensation for war damage.

In 1949 work started on the Langton-Canada scheme, partly to restore war damage and partly to improve access to the North docks. The scheme involved constructing a new Langton river entrance, widening the Canada-Brocklebank passage and modernising the adjacent dock area. This proved far more expensive than originally estimated, costing about £20 million, and in itself produced no direct additional revenue. Another new development, on the other hand, the construction in the late 1950s of a new terminal at Tranmere to serve the Shell refinery at Ellesmere Port (costing about £4 million) was a profitable source of income.

To meet the cost of its capital expenditure, in 1958 the Board issued £10 million of 5¾% stock 1976/78 at 97.

In April 1963 the new General Manager, Mr. (later Sir) Clifford Dove, recommended that the Board should obtain outside advice on its finances and merchant bankers, Baring Brothers & Co. Ltd., were retained. The position at this time was that the Board had used some £9 million of reserves to finance capital expenditure. The sinking fund had extinguished some £14 million of debt. There were four debenture stocks outstanding:

3½% 1975/85 issued between 1934 and 1938—£1,976,276
3¼% 1975/85 issued between 1934 and 1937—£3,927,400
3¼% 1970/80 issued in 1935—£9,759,621
5¾% 1976/78 issued in 1958—£10,000,000

Additionally there were short term borrowings of £36,956,143, amounting to 56.8% of the total debt.

Barings were asked to advise on:

(a) (in the broadest sense) their assessment of the financial position of the Board both present and future, with particular regard to capital structure
(b) action to be taken as to future borrowings, i.e. stock or bonds, terms and timing.

Barings declared themselves in wholehearted agreement with the report of the Government-appointed Rochdale Committee (see p. 13) regarding finance and strongly recommended that fullest consideration should be given to adopting the suggestions made.

> We appreciate that assessing the feasibility of accepting the recommendations in full and planning the timing of putting such recommendations into effect will involve the preparation of estimates of the incidence of cost on annual revenues, particularly on the question of depreciation on a replacement cost basis, and that this will take time. We believe, however, that at this stage it will be time well spent if for no other reason than that a fundamental appreciation can be made of the value of the assets in use, of the revenues required to meet their due replacement and of

the need to ensure that at all times they are economically employed.

On the funding of the Board's capital expenditure Barings said:

It is appreciated that, whether changes are made or not in providing depreciation on a replacement basis and in the application of Sinking Fund monies to repayment of capital, the hard core of permanent finance required by the Board must continue to be provided by loan capital. Furthermore, it is incumbent on the Board to raise such capital in as economic a manner as possible bearing in mind particularly that in effect the objects of the Board and their financing can be regarded as substantially permanent.

It is the present practice of the Board, and has been we understand over many years, to raise the bulk of its financial requirements on a comparatively short term basis. Arising out of this policy the Board has found itself in the position of performing the functions of a Savings Bank.

That a service is done for the community is beyond question; that this service is for the ultimate benefit of the Port and its users and that it is the best means of providing hard core finance is in our view open to serious doubt.

They accordingly suggested a programme of borrowing £32 million for periods ranging from 20 to 30 years, over the four years from 1964 to 1968. Thereafter they indicated that it might be appropriate to issue debenture stocks every five years for 30-year periods. They encouraged the Board to put their suggestions, if accepted, into effect as soon as possible.

The board accepted Barings' proposals in principle and it was agreed in March 1964 to make three issues of stock as follows:

27 September 1964—£12.5 million 1985/90
1st January 1966—£10 million 1990/95
1st January 1968—£8 million 1990/95

In the event, an issue of £5 million 6.625% 1990/93 stock at 99.5 was made in February 1965 and was heavily oversubscribed. Bonds falling due for renewal in March, July and September 1965 were paid off. Another stock issue of £15 million 6¾% 1992/95 was made in December 1965, also at 99.5 and the bonds falling due for renewal in

January and March 1966 were also paid off. However, 94% of the December 1965 stock had been left with the underwriters and it was decided to postpone the issue of further stock until the autumn of 1967; meanwhile offers to renew existing bonds were to be made. In the event, market conditions remained such that the policy of renewing bonds continued from the September 1966 quarter to the March 1968 quarter. Renewals were usually for five years at rates varying between 6¾% and 7¼% and proportions renewed varied between 25% and 50% of the amounts falling due.

Chapter 2
POLITICAL BACKGROUND

The efficiency of its ports is important to the United Kingdom as an island trading nation and over the years many commissions, committees and experts, official and unofficial, have inquired into various aspects of the health of the ports industry. Ports have also often been the subject of political contention. The 1960s was a period of lively activity on both these fronts.

In March 1961 the Conservative Minister of Transport, Ernest Marples (M.P. for Wallasey, a constituency which includes part of Birkenhead docks) set up a Committee of Inquiry of five persons chaired by Viscount Rochdale with the terms of reference:

> To consider to what extent the major docks and harbours of Great Britain are adequate to meet present and future national needs; whether the methods of working can be improved; and to make recommendations.

As their report,[1] presented to Parliament in September 1962, records, they spent 18 days visiting ports including Antwerp, Hamburg and Rotterdam on the Continent, as well as taking written and oral evidence from many bodies and individuals. The report has always been regarded as a comprehensive and authoritative description and critique of the state of the ports industry at the beginning of the 1960s.

The Rochdale Committee's principal recommendation was the establishment of a National Ports Authority with statutory powers to control investment and to supervise in a non-operational role a properly planned programme of port development to be concentrated at selected major ports on the main estuaries. General recommendations having a bearing on Liverpool included that 'after covering working expenses, ports should aim at providing out of revenue for interest on loans, depreciation of assets on a replacement cost basis, taxation and some margin for reserves to meet contingencies and to help finance minor improvements'.[2]

In commenting on the constitution of trust ports they said: 'We agree that users generally should have a substantial representation but we are convinced that regular payers of rates and dues should not be in the majority. True as it may be that local users have a direct interest in the efficient daily running of a port, we believe that divided loyalties must sometimes make it difficult for them to take a dispassionate long-term view of financial problems'.[3] They did not, however, make any formal recommendations on this matter.

They advocated the setting up of new port trusts, for example to administer the ports of Tees and Hartlepool[4] and the Humber,[5] but made no recommendations as to how these port trusts should be constituted.

On Liverpool specifically, the Rochdale report said the Mersey Docks and Harbour Board should assume responsibility for Garston and Bromborough docks (owned respectively by the British Transport Docks Board and Unilever);[6] that for the time being effort at both Liverpool and Manchester should generally be concentrated on making the most of existing facilities, and in particular the Langton-Canada scheme at Liverpool, rather than on major developments;[7] and that while no amalgamation of the ports of Liverpool and Manchester was desirable for the time being, the proposed National Ports Authority should keep the position under review.[8]

An interesting aspect of the Rochdale Report is the paucity of references to containerisation. Six paragraphs in the chapter 'Recent Developments in Cargo Handling' in a report of 659 paragraphs refer in terms to containers and containerisation, but the Committee's generally cautious approach to this technological development which was to lead to a revolution in shipping and consequently to port operations within the next few years is reflected in this passage from the Report:

> In some of the evidence we have received the suggestion has been made that we have entered a new era in the physical layout of docks and harbours. It is contended, for example, that the carriage of far more general cargo in containers and unit loads, coupled possibly with the mechanised transfer of goods from ship to shore and thence to inland terminals, could drastically reduce

> the time spent by ships alongside (if they needed to come alongside at all) and also the time for which goods have to remain within the port area. Indeed, a stage might even be reached at which containers are transferred from ship to inland terminal in one continuous operation, thereby eliminating altogether port transit sheds or warehouses. In such a port bulk cargo would be dealt with equally expeditiously, but at specialised berths equipped with specialised machinery. We do not believe it is possible to judge how realistic such ideas are or how soon and to what extent our major ports might be converted; we feel sure, however, that these ideas should engage the most serious attention of port authorities and of the National Ports Authority.[9]

Unlike many reports of official commissions, the Rochdale Report was not put on a shelf and allowed to gather dust. In 1964 the Harbours Act was passed, giving effect to many of the principal recommendations of the Report, though not always in quite the form recommended. In particular, instead of establishing a National Ports Authority with powers 'to safeguard the national, as well as the local, interest in port development'[10] by controlling major capital investment by port authorities, this power was given to the Minister of Transport[11] and the National Ports Council established by the Act was given only advisory functions in this key area.[12]

In parallel with the restriction on capital expenditure over a figure fixed by subsequent regulations at £500,000,[13] later raised to £1 million,[14] the Harbours Act 1964 introduced new forms of government assistance to port authorities by way of loan and grant to execute harbour works and to acquire plant and equipment.

The National Ports Council, whose first Chairman was Viscount Rochdale, themselves commissioned a report from consultants Touche Ross to determine whether, as the U.K. ports industry had always contended, Continental ports enjoyed financial advantages not available to U.K. ports and were thereby able to draw trade away from the U.K. The consultants studied the position of four Continental ports, Antwerp, Dunkirk, Hamburg and Rotterdam, and compared them with Liverpool, London and Southampton. They concluded that the four Continental ports enjoyed major advantages, receiving 'massive financial aid' from central and local governments who regarded the ports as 'a vital part of their overall economy rather than as commercial enterprises in their own right' (words which imply a trenchant criticism of the policy of the British government). In addition to direct financial aids, all the Continental ports received benefits from central or local government in the form of services provided free for which U.K. ports had to pay, for example, dredging of the port approaches and policing. In the case of Rotterdam and Hamburg (both estimated to be incurring large deficits on port operations, assessed at £6 million annually in the case of Hamburg), the port accounts were included in the city accounts and thus their deficits were effectively written off.

Touche Ross reckoned that had Liverpool enjoyed these advantages, charges on ships and goods could have been reduced by from 13% to 51% according to which Continental port was compared, or alternatively that the Board's results over past years would have been substantially better.

Touche Ross repeated the study to include data to the end of 1973 and reported again to the National Ports Council in August 1974. They arrived at basically the same conclusions, though Liverpool was not one of the U.K. ports chosen for comparison, Bristol being substituted. Neither report had any perceptible influence on U.K. Government policy.

One particular aspect of port operations which over the years attracted a plethora of reports was dock labour. Under the National Dock Labour Scheme 1947[15] loading and unloading of cargo in most U.K. ports including Liverpool could be performed only by dockers on a register maintained by the National Dock Labour Board. This Board was jointly controlled by the two sides of the industry, employers and trades union, and local administration of the Board's functions was delegated to local boards composed of equal numbers of representatives of employers and dockers. In ensuing years numerous reports were commissioned by Ministers of Labour on the workings of the scheme, of which the Leggett Report 1951,[16] the Devlin Reports 1956[17] and 1964/6,[18] the Scamp Report 1967[19] and the Pearson Report 1970[20] are only a few examples.[21]

Essentially, dock work was insecure and spasmodic. Due to the fluctuating nature of ship arrivals and departures, there was not always sufficient work for all the dockers in any port. Under the Scheme a docker who attended for work but for whom none was available was paid attendance money, with a guaranteed weekly wage if his earnings and attendance money fell below a minimum settled from time to time by negotiation. On the other hand, as the number of men on the register was restricted, there were occasions when the number of dockers was insufficient for the work available, with consequent delays to shipping.

Though some dockers were engaged on a weekly basis, it was still essentially a casual job for the majority. Most dockers were in 'the pool', required to attend and be allocated to employers as and when they required labour. This continuing element of casual employment had been considered by the first of the reports cited above, the Leggett Report 1951, which recommended the extension as far as possible of permanent employment. In 1961 the National Joint Council of the Port Transport Industry, the industry's negotiating body, declared that further decasualisation was desirable and issued a directive to all local joint committees calling on them to study and report by the 1st January 1962 on the practicability, in relation to their area, of a substantial advance towards decasualisation; in return it was expected that restrictive practices, especially those inhibiting mobility of labour, would be abolished. This directive was not complied with by the prescribed date, negotiations being complicated in Liverpool by the existence of two rival unions representing dockers—the union recognised by the employers, the Transport and General Workers Union, and the unrecognised National Association of Stevedores and Dockers, the so-called Blue Union, who were not represented on the local Dock Labour Board.

The Rochdale Report included a section headed 'Decasualisation',[22] urging the parties to press ahead with arrangements for the greatest possible degree of decasualisation within the Scheme. However, negotiations dragged on inconclusively while labour relations in the industry continued to deteriorate and in 1964 the Minister of Labour appointed another committee under the distinguished Law Lord, Lord Devlin (who had held an inquiry eight years previously), to inquire into, *inter alia*, 'decasualisation and the causes of dissension in the port transport industry and other matters affecting efficiency'.

Though not formally asked to make any recommendations, Lord Devlin concluded that the 1961 national directive still provided the best line of approach to reform of industrial relations in the docks, but that the objective should be the engagement on a weekly basis of all registered dockers. A procedure was proposed in his Report[23] whereby the objectives of the directive could be progressively negotiated, with the ultimate sanction of a scheme to be imposed by Government.

The Docks and Harbours Act 1966 gave effect to some of Lord Devlin's proposals, imposing on port authorities the function of licensing employers of dock labour, with the aim of weeding out the less efficient. Ports were also to draw up and implement schemes for improving amenities, such as canteens and locker rooms, for the dockers.

This was by no means the final word on the matter of labour relations in the port industry, but its working out and subsequent developments, notably the Aldington-Jones Report (or, as some prefer, the Jones-Aldington Report) of 1974, will be considered chronologically in their relation to the wider history of the Port of Liverpool in a later chapter.

Meanwhile the election of a Labour Government in April 1966 presaged a fundamental upheaval for the ports industry. In their election manifesto the Labour Party declared:

> In order to speed the flow of exports we shall reorganise and modernise the nation's ports on the basis of a strong National Ports Authority and publicly-owned regional port authorities. Within the ports we shall end inefficiencies and delays in cargo-handling and help to end the chaos of the casual system by making each port authority ultimately responsible for all port operations within its area, including stevedoring, and by extending the present valuable experiment of joint participation.

Nevertheless, this policy was not pursued with any urgency. In July 1967 the Ministry of Transport circulated a consultative document to interested parties proposing the 1st January 1970 as the target date for nationalisation based on a National Ports Authority and eight regional port authorities, with Liverpool part of a region extending from the Solway Firth to Anglesey. When no mention was made of port nationalisation in the Queen's Speech at the beginning of the 1968/9 Parliamentary session, a group of Labour back bench M.P.s signed a motion criticising the omission. The Prime Minister, Mr. Harold Wilson, responded by promising a White Paper 'soon'.[24] This was in fact published at the end of January 1969,[25] but a further 10 months elapsed before the legislative process began with the publication of the Ports Bill which the Government aimed to get passed by mid-1970. The Bill proposed the nationalisation of all major ports under a National Ports Authority, which was to assume responsibility for the debts of the port authorities on their existing terms as to interest and repayment.

In January 1970 a preparatory committee was established, chaired by Mr. (later Sir) Peter Parker, a businessman much favoured by Labour governments for membership of nationalised bodies;[26] he was thus Chairman designate of the proposed National Ports Authority. He and other designated members of the proposed Authority made a tour of the ports which were to vest in it, including Liverpool, to assess the resources that would be available, particularly the managerial resources.

However, in May the Prime Minister announced the calling of a general election on the 18th June, and in the consequent curtailment of the Government's legislative programme the Ports Bill was abandoned, even though it had made considerable progress and could, had it been politically expedient, have been pushed through to Royal Assent before Parliament was prorogued.

During the debate on the 29th April 1970 on the report stage of the Ports Bill, Mr. Michael Heseltine, Conservative Opposition spokesman on Transport matters, had described the Mersey Docks and Harbour Board as 'probably the one insoluble financial problem . . . this is the one area where one cannot see a means of solving its financial difficulties purely because of the funding of its long term capital stock'.[27]

In the election a Conservative Government, headed by Mr. Edward Heath, was elected and any possibility of nationalisation was killed off once and, so far as one can foresee, for all. As a consequence the Harbours Act 1964, which would have been repealed, and the National Ports Council, which would have been abolished, were reprieved.

Chapter 3
1965–1970

On the 2nd August 1965 the Mersey Docks and Harbour Board was reconstituted, its numbers being reduced from 28, as it had been since 1858, to a maximum of 18—12 user members (six representing shipowners and six representing traders of whom at least two were to be representatives of exporters), 4 members appointed by the Minister of Transport as previously, with power for the Board to co-opt up two further members.[1] This power was exercised immediately to co-opt the director-general since 1962, Mr. Clifford Dove, the first executive officer of the Board to be a member of it.

The first Chairman of the newly constituted Board was Mr. Morton Duff Oliphant, a director of Tate and Lyle, the sugar manufacturers, and also of the Board's bankers, Martins Bank (the Liverpool-based bank since taken over by Barclays Bank). His first report, published in December 1965 with the annual accounts for July 1964 to July 1965, had a notably confident tone.

> It has become almost customary to announce new records each year in both the tonnages of ships and cargo, the latter now standing at an all time record total of well over 28.25 million tons. We believe that our ability to maintain these records is completely dependent upon the expansion of our facilities, which is the spur to urge on our development plans. Such a figure is only a stage in our ultimate capability.

He announced the initiation of feasibility studies to extend the dock system northwards from Gladstone Dock.[2] Contrary to the view expressed in the Rochdale Report that Liverpool should concentrate its effort on making the most of its existing facilities, the National Ports Council had supported this proposed development in the Interim Plan for some major ports which they had recently published. This extension was estimated to cost £36 million and was designed to provide 14 new deep-water berths, the first of which was forecast to come into commission in early 1971. This was in addition to a programme of modernising 23 existing berths, including berths in Toxteth, Harrington and Kings Docks in the South Docks system, at a cost of about £5 million, and plans to deepen the river and deepen and straighten the main channel into the port to facilitate access for larger tankers going to the Tranmere oil terminal.

Negotiations were in progress to acquire Garston and Bromborough Docks as recommended in the Rochdale Report, with a target date of 1968 in the case of Garston.

The Chairman referred to the Devlin Report as 'a tragic tale brilliantly told'. There had been some 200 working days in the period of about 18 months covered by the statement when there was insufficient labour in the Port. At this time the Board did not engage in cargo-handling, which was carried out by private stevedoring companies, and therefore employed no registered dock workers (except to a limited extent in their warehouses), though the Board had signalled an intention of starting a cargo handling operation. Nevertheless it was, of course, much concerned to see the successful implementation of Lord Devlin's recommendations and was discussing with the Employers Association of the Port of Liverpool, representing the Port's stevedoring employers, a scheme to concentrate their respective areas of operation to facilitate such implementation.

Summarising the annual accounts, the Chairman said 'Finally on our financial state; this is good. Only 2 years ago we were running a heavy deficit. This year we are able to show an overall surplus of £1.5 million after payment of £3.2 million in interest charges on our borrowed monies and contributing over £.75 million to the Sinking Fund'. On depreciation he said:

> We do not like raising charges for we are not a profit-making concern. We have to make enough surplus to pay for one thing only, interest at a rate sufficient to make the public continue to invest with us sufficient money to carry on the work of the port. The value of an undertaking must be maintained and this involves providing for depreciation of our assets at replacement cost, a practice which has not been observed in port accounting in the past. To do this in full at one bite would involve increasing our charges by some 20% which would damage the national economy.

> We are therefore moving towards full replacement cost depreciation by stages, so that shipowners and traders have time to re-adjust themselves to the necessary measures. To do otherwise would be to drive trade away from Liverpool to other ports. I cannot believe that would be considered by anyone to be in the interests of the Port of Liverpool, or of any of the many people and activities depending on a busy Merseyside for their contribution to the national economic health.

He also noted what he described as 'a modest start' in the policy of funding the Board's short term debt by the 'issue of £5 million debenture stock 1990–1993 at $6\frac{3}{4}$% issued at 99.5. That the yield to redemption of £6 13s 3d per cent was only some 4s 6d more than comparable Government stock, coupled with the oversubscription of some 8 times, shows that our credit is high'.

The Board made another surplus exceeding £1 million in the financial year ended July 1966 but, as the Chairman noted, the strike of British seamen from the 16th May to the 1st July had cost the Board between £250,000 and £300,000 in revenue.

The proposed development at Seaforth had received statutory approval in the Mersey Docks and Harbour Board (Seaforth Works) Act 1966, though the formal consent of the Minister of Transport required under the Harbours Act 1964 was not given until March 1967.

Shortage of labour was still causing delays to shipping. As against an approved register of 14,500, the number had fallen below 13,000. In April 1966 the Board had started its own cargo-handling operation on five berths in the north docks system.

To accommodate the container traffic, now increasingly replacing some of the general cargo traffic which had traditionally used the port, the Gladstone graving dock (opened in 1913 to accommodate the largest trans-Atlantic passenger liners) was adapted as a container berth as an interim facility until the new Seaforth development became available. Though it had a heavy crane, it was not fully equipped for container-handling and was not therefore commissioned until May 1968, and for several months thereafter was used only by small vessels. When this facility started to be used by larger vessels on the Atlantic trade, Hornby dock was adapted as an additional temporary container berth for the short-sea trades.

The effect of containerisation was shown by the decision of the Australian trade, which had traditionally used Liverpool for the import of wool for the Yorkshire textile industry, to route their containers through one U.K. port in Southern England more convenient for the vessels to proceed to Continental ports. In the second half of 1966 the previous heavy shortages of labour began to turn into surpluses, often of 1,000 men. Though Liverpool's register was 2,500 below the authorised level and the average age was getting disquietingly high, recruitment was stopped as the National Dock Labour Board imposed a national standstill.

The financial year July 1966 to July 1967 was significantly less successful than the previous year, the surplus being down by approximately 50% to £750,000 which, as the Chairman pointed out, was far less than was needed to cover replacement cost depreciation as the National Ports Council was advocating in line with the Rochdale Report.

The proposals[3] by the Minister of Transport, Mrs. Barbara Castle, in July 1967 to nationalise the ports with a target date of the 1st January 1970 by means of a three-tier structure (National Ports Authority, eight Regional Port Authorities and the ports themselves) were criticised by the Chairman in his 1967 statement. He doubted whether any economies would accrue from such a structure and feared that the consequences would be 'over-centralisation of control and an absence of competition leading to higher charges and thus a loss of trade to Continental ports'. He added that not all his Board colleagues agreed with this view; the matter had been debated by the Board on the 7th August 1967, when two of the Government-nominated members had proposed a resolution welcoming the Government's proposals and hoping for their earliest implementation. Because of these nationalisation proposals, discussions for the acquisition of Garston and Bromborough docks were temporarily (and, as it turned out, permanently) shelved with the concurrence of the National Ports Council as all three dock systems were proposed for nationalisation.

Decasualisation of dock labour pursuant to the Devlin Report was introduced in September 1967, bringing on a six-week official strike in Liverpool.

At the request of the National Ports Council, the Board altered its accounting year to the calendar year and therefore produced a six months' account for the second half of 1967. This recorded a loss of over £1 million, attributed chiefly to the effect of the six-week strike, not only because of the loss of ships and goods during the strike period, but also due to the residual effects of quay congestion and ship delays described by the Chairman as 'appalling'.

Estimates submitted to the Board at the beginning of 1968 forecast that £28 million would be required in 1968 and 1969 to finance capital works (Seaforth £15 million and other projects £13 million), in addition to £8 million which would be required to pay off maturing bonds, assuming a 40% renewal. Taking account of available investments, projected port modernisation grants (£3 million) and a forecast surplus from revenue of £3 million (which in the event turned out to be a £3 million deficit), the estimate was that £26 million would need to be borrowed. Following discussion with Barings, the National Ports Council and the Ministry of Transport, the Board decided to apply for £13.5 million in loans under the Harbours Act 1964 and to issue £15 million of debenture stock.

Though they had been advised in 1966 that the Government's nationalisation proposals should not affect the Board's ability to borrow, in fact in August 1968 Barings and the Board's brokers, Pember and Boyle, were told that the Treasury and the Bank of England, in consultation with the Ministry of Transport, would not permit the Board to issue debenture stock in view of the Government's intention to nationalise the ports. The Bank suggested that the Board should meet its foreseeable needs by yearling bonds, but Barings persuaded them to go so far as to approve the issue of longer-term bonds. (It is of interest to note that the Port of London Authority had also been refused permission to issue debenture stock.) Therefore, though it was entering a period of heavy capital expenditure, the Board had to continue borrowing short-term. In October 1968 it successfully invited applications for new money secured by bonds in the sum of £8.5 million at 8% for periods of two to five years.

Attempts by the Board throughout this period to raise its charges to improve its deteriorating finances met resistance from Government, whose policy was by exhortation or control to restrain price increases to counter inflationary pressures. In August 1965 application was made to increase charges by 10% from the 2nd December. This request was referred back for further consideration and agreement was subsequently reached that, instead of a 10% increase in 1965, 20% should be added at 5% over each of the next four years. However, the

Government's six-month price freeze from July 1966 to 1967, followed by six months of 'severe restraint', prevented implementation in 1966 and 1967. In August 1967 permission for a further $3\frac{1}{2}$% increase was sought in addition to the 10% due in respect of the previous two years: the Ministry consented only to a $3\frac{1}{2}$% increase effective from October 1967. A further cut-back was applied when permission for an increase was sought in July 1968.

Under the Harbours Act 1964, port users had a right of appeal to the National Ports Council against port charges. The restraining effect of this was more indirect than direct since only one appeal was ever made against the Board's charges. This was an appeal against the charges on the export of malt and the chartered accountant whom the N.P.C. appointed to hold an inquiry said in his report 'It is unreasonable that the Board should have regard only to their own finances in this exercise of their functions'.[4]

The deficit on the revenue account continued into 1968, to the tune of £1.226 million, attributed again to the backlog of the dockers' strike and subsequent strikes. Another effect of the decasualisation of dock labour was to cause some of the private stevedoring companies in the Port, especially those with no tie to particular shipping companies, to review their position. Scruttons (Cargo Services) Ltd. and Freight Conveyors Mersey Ports Stevedoring Limited approached the Board, and their businesses were taken over by the Board in 1969 with consequent extension of its cargo-handling operations into berths in the South Docks and Birkenhead. The Board now employed one-fifth of the dock labour in the Port.

In May 1969 the Board announced a feasibility study in collaboration with Liverpool University into the possibility of constructing an oil terminal 11 miles off-shore in Liverpool Bay, in the form of a man-made island capable of taking the megaton tankers then being contemplated by some oil companies, with storage facilities for 1.25 million tons of oil connected by pipelines to the shore.

Commenting on the Government's 1969 White Paper on port nationalisation, the Chairman welcomed the dropping of the three-tier proposals and the reversion to estuarial groupings. He still, nevertheless, called for the dropping of nationalisation:

> Nearly all the large ports are Public Trusts already: as such the Minister of Transport has a very large measure of control over

them. They cannot build major works without his consent, they cannot raise their charges without his consent, and they cannot raise money without Treasury consent. No more control is necessary or desirable in the interests of competition either between themselves or with Continental Ports.

In the summer of 1969 Barings sought Bank of England approval to offer to renew the £3.4 million bonds falling due in September for five to seven years, but were advised that after consultation with the Treasury, permission could only be given to renew for 18 months (subsequently extended to 30 months) in order to avoid a commitment to a high interest rate which would be inherited on nationalisation. The Bank had confirmed to Barings that they were looking at the question as a Government agency rather than in their function of maintaining an orderly market. Barings argued strongly that this was unreasonable, since the Board had to take commercial decisions in the light of existing circumstances which were in any case largely of the Government's own creation, and nationalisation was only a possibility. If the financial arrangements of the Board had to be made purely on the basis of possible nationalisation, this could be to the considerable detriment of the Board should nationalisation not materialise. Cassandra could not have been more prescient.[5]

In September 1969 renewals, together with a small sum of new money accepted, left a shortfall of some £1.5 million less than the total amount of bonds maturing and, when the January 1970 renewals were dealt with, new money was also raised from institutions to cover this shortfall.

Forecasts before the Board in April showed that if the Board was allowed to renew the £6 million of bonds falling due in January 1971 for only two years, it would be faced with maturities of £8 million in January 1973. The Chairman felt that the Bank of England should be pressed to allow a longer period of renewal of the January 1971 bonds.

A further report to the Board from the Chief Accountant in July 1969 showed the Board's worsening position over recent years when the revenue surplus after charging interest and depreciation had declined from £1.5 million in July 1966 to a deficit of £1.78 million in December 1969. During this period the debt had increased by £11 million and interest rates had increased from $6\frac{3}{4}\%$ to $9\frac{3}{4}\%$, over

£22 million of the debt being at a rate of 8% or more by December 1969.

The forecast for the next five years to December 1974 was that in each year the operating surplus would be exceeded by the charge for interest, which would rise from £4.1 million (net) in 1969 to £10.75 million in 1974. Meanwhile the estimate of the cost of Seaforth, £36 million in 1965, had risen to £39 million.

In July 1969 Mr. Oliphant resigned from the Board and Mr. J. C. Taylor, a director of Cunard, was elected as Chairman in his place. His first and, as it turned out, last annual statement, published in April 1970, was as downbeat as that of Mr. Oliphant in 1965 had been upbeat. He started with an expression of regret that the Port's fortunes had failed to improve after the losses of 1967 and 1968; the overall deficit for 1969 was £1.78 million. To rectify these continuing losses the Board had applied to the Department of Transport for permission to increase its principal charges by 10% from the 1st October 1969 but in the event the increase was delayed by two months. The losses were forecast to continue into 1970. The Chairman referred to the Touche Ross report comparing the finances of four major Continental ports with three English ports, whose implications, he commented, were 'there for all to see'. But for a revaluation of the Board's land by £17.667 million (based by the Board's Estate Manager on the value of adjoining and adjacent land reflected in an increase in the reserves) the Board's Balance Sheet as at 31st December 1969 would have looked even worse.

A constant refrain in the Chairman's statements from 1966 onwards was the detrimental effect on the Board's finances of labour problems—labour shortages resulting, for example, from the backlog of trade created by the seamen's strike of 1966 or the failure in 1969 to agree on how to recruit additional dockers as had been decided upon by the National Dock Labour Board nationally and locally; the six-week dockers' strike on decasualisation in 1967 (estimated to have cost between three-quarters of a million pounds and one million pounds); and political strikes in 1968.

The progressive containerisation led to insecurity for the dockers. Whilst the continuing conventional trade necessitated a substantial labour force, there was an understandable reluctance (in an industry where the labour force had an effective veto on recruitment through their joint control of the National Dock Labour Board) to agree to the taking on of new dockers when in the medium term containerisation was likely to lead to a substantial reduction in work for dockers. In 1968 Container Base Federation, who were developing a national network of facilities for container-handling, planned a base at Aintree, only three miles or so from Liverpool docks. The Federation had signed a national agreement with the Transport and General Workers Union under which work at their bases was allocated to the Union's Transport and Commercial Group. Recruitment for the Aintree base was to start in May 1969, ready for its opening in June. The Liverpool Docks Section of the T.G.W.U. took exception to the agreement that had been signed by their Union's national officials and demanded that Aintree should be reserved for registered dock workers. They also objected to the terms and conditions being offered to employees at Aintree, which were in line with those at the Federation's other bases but reckoned by the dockers to be inferior to those applying at the Port's Gladstone container terminal.

Container Base Federation refused to abrogate unilaterally their agreement with the Union. Industrial action, in the form of unofficial strikes and a ban on all containers from the docks, forced the Federation and the Union to negotiate a special agreement for Aintree, giving the work to registered dock workers.

Another important factor relating to industrial relations in this period was the rise of the shop steward movement in the docks. This had been advocated by the Devlin Committee as a means of improving communications between employers, dockers and full-time officials of the Union.[6] This was a policy that the T.G.W.U. national leadership fostered with enthusiasm, despite the misgivings of some of its local full time officials. In their 1969 report, the Employers Association of the Port of Liverpool devoted a special section to the issue. They said:

> The shop steward system was introduced into the Liverpool Docks at the beginning of 1968; twelve months later shop stewards had effectively taken all real power from the hands of their union officials and the District Committee. This development appears to be in accord with the new policy of the T.G.W.U.: retiring full-time union officials are generally not being replaced. During the year, the position of shop stewards as a policy-making force became formalised by the establishment of a Shop Stewards' Executive Committee with appropriate officers.

> Discussions have taken place with a view to creating a small number of 'senior shop stewards' as full-time salaried appointments.
>
> At the present time, many of the leaders of the 1967 strike are at the centre of the shop steward movement, but their position is increasingly challenged by younger or more militant men. This appears to be an inevitable development of the abrogation of formal union authority and responsibility, which set the pattern for a shift of power to those prepared to challenge the status quo. Whilst the experience of the more established shop steward leaders has so far enabled them to remain in control, they are increasingly driven to take up or defend extreme positions as the result of irresponsible acts of a number of their colleagues, who appear to believe that the principal function of a shop steward is to harass management.
>
> The immediate future is gloomy, and the forecast in 1967 by national and local union officials that the introduction of shop stewards would be an aid to stability and peace, has been sadly and massively proved wrong.

The Association's 1970 Report recorded that 'there was virtually no change in the position reported in respect of last year. It would seem that at present the real power on the Trade Union side in the port rests in the hands of shop stewards'.

However, despite the growth of containerisation there was still strong demand for conventional break-bulk cargo-handling facilities, and the shortage of dock labour was a serious constraint on improving the port's throughput. Though agreement had been reached for limited recruitment to replace men leaving the register, the employers and union could not agree in the Local Dock Labour Board on how to select the authorised recruits.

On the Ports Bill Mr. Taylor said:

> As a Board we are not in favour of nationalisation and are not persuaded that this policy is the right one. We believe it is essential to retain local autonomy for ports in order to deal effectively with local problems.
>
> We are confident that given the necessary financial assistance to develop our facilities, we could provide more satisfactorily the full range and high level of services required by our customers.

Three weeks after this statement was published with the Board's accounts for 1969, the Government withdrew the Ports Bill (a case, however, of *post hoc* and not *propter hoc*) and the Board had to reassess its situation as an autonomous public trust.

Chapter 4
THE CRISIS BREAKS

Within six weeks of the election of the Conservative Government in June 1970, the Board's Chairman Mr. Joseph Taylor, and Director General Mr. Robert Edwards (who had succeeded Mr. Dove in 1969), met the new Minister of Transport (later redesignated Minister for Transport Industries) Mr. John Peyton, to express their anxiety over the Board's liquidity position. This, Mr. Taylor explained, was caused by the increasing burden of interest payments resulting from the large amount of capital being invested in the new Seaforth development, and also the high interest rates both on new borrowing and the refinancing of low interest loans falling due for redemption. Mr. Edwards said that in his opinion Seaforth alone could not be expected to solve all the Board's problems and that rationalisation of the existing dock system would also be required. However, Mr. Taylor and Mr. Edwards expressed optimism about the Port's profitability in the longer term, based partly on the planned off-shore terminal to replace the Tranmere oil terminal, described by Mr. Edwards as 'an important and pleasing prospect'.

Mr. Taylor said the Board would probably need to borrow about £30 million over the next five years, and it would greatly help if it could borrow at less than the current high standard interest rates, drawing attention to the advantageous financial terms available to Continental ports as recorded in the Touche Ross report to the National Ports Council.

The Minister responded by referring to 'the difficult state of the national economy' (some things never change) and said it would not be for him to reduce interest rates on loans but was for the Treasury and perhaps the Cabinet to consider. He also suggested that the Board should review its constitution to lessen shipowner representation.

It was agreed that the Board should appoint financial consultants from a list of four or five firms to be suggested by the Ministry, who should be asked to report by Christmas.

The meeting was reported to the board on the 10th August and the appointment of the accountancy firm of Binder Hamlyn and Co. was confirmed, and subsequently the following comprehensive terms of reference were agreed.

1. To assist the Board in the management of their cash resources in the period to 30th December, 1970 involving:
   a) assistance in the preparation of detailed cash flow forecasts;
   b) examination of the cash flow problems which will arise in the period;
   c) consideration of advice on ways in which cash resources may be increased.
2. To assist in the preparation of a financial plan for the 5 years to the end of 1975 involving:
   a) a review of the method of preparation of and the assumptions underlying the Board's budget for 1971 and the estimates of the revenue account for the following 4 years and advice thereon;
   b) consideration of, and advice on, steps which the Board might take to improve forecast revenue results during this period;
   c) assisting the Board in the preparation of revised budget and revenue account estimates;
   d) in consultation with Barings, advising the Board on whether the Board's capital liabilities need to be reduced and, if so, on the extent of the required reduction;
   e) assisting the Board in the preparation of a financial plan, incorporating the revised interest charges;
   f) reporting to the Board on the assumptions underlying the financial plan, and on the accounting bases and calculations of the forecasts.
3. To assist Barings, as may be required, in the formulation of a scheme for reconstruction of the Board's capital and to recommend thereon.
4. To advise and assist the Board, as may be required, in solving any financial problems which arise in the implementation of

> the Scheme for reconstruction and in the conduct of the Board's operations during the period of implementation.

At the beginning of September 1970 the Board routinely offered terms for the renewal for two to five years of £993,831 of bonds falling due at the end of September, and applications were invited for the loan of new money on similar terms.

The first results of Binder Hamlyn's inquiries were contained in a letter of the 10th September which stated their preliminary opinion that, based on the forecast losses for 1970 and the next five years, aggregating £7 million, the necessity for re-financing £28.6 million of capital debt and the contemplated capital expenditure of £30 million by the end of 1973, it was unlikely that the Board would find itself able to borrow, without a guarantee from a third party, to replace the £6.2 million of bonds falling due on the 1st January 1971. They added:

> Moreover we see dangers in allowing the present position to develop to the point where new funds are raised without sufficient certainty that they will be repaid on the due dates. Taking company law as a parallel, this might involve Board Members in personal liability.
>
> If we understand the position correctly, it may be necessary to request a moratorium to delay repayment of the £6.2m of Bonds. This might precipitate the appointment of a receiver to look after the interests of these bondholders, which would inevitably have a serious effect on the future development of the port. For this reason, we think that you should consider applying to the Minister of Transport for financial assistance. The figures required to support a detailed application will not be ready for about a month but in view of the short time available we think it advisable that a preliminary approach should be made as soon as possible. At the same time, further thought should be given to the nature of the financial assistance required.
>
> We also think it essential that urgent consideration be given to means of improving the revenue results of the Board over the next few years through increasing revenue and decreasing costs, since proposals for restoring the Board to viability must, in our view, form an important part of any application for financial assistance.

This devastatingly forthright letter precipitated the calling of a meeting of the Chairman, Deputy Chairman and senior officials of the

Board with the partner of Binder Hamlyn in charge of their investigation and Peter Baring of Baring Bros. At this meeting the decision was taken to suspend the offer to renew the bonds falling due at the end of the month and the offer to borrow new money. The suggestion that the Government should give a confidential guarantee of the September bonds, both capital and interest, to allow time for the formulation of orderly plans, was floated with civil servants at the Transport Ministry, but they replied that any form of Government support would have to be made public.

In the light of advice received from leading City Solicitors, Slaughter and May, on the personal responsibility of board members to the effect that if the board was in doubt as to its ability to repay the bonds whose renewal it was inviting, failure to make full disclosure of its financial problems could constitute a breach of the Prevention of Fraud (Investments) Act 1958, it was decided to return money already received. This drastic step (which led to protests from bondholders insistent on wishing to renew their bonds) was confirmed by the board at a meeting on the 14th September.

The Board's officials and advisers embarked on an intensive series of meetings with civil servants of the Ministry which continued throughout the ensuing weeks as the crisis unfolded. On the 16th September it was agreed that the Board should prepare a statement of its financial position and a plan for remedial action which was sent to the Ministry the next day. This forecast—on the assumption that charges were increased by 25%, the South Docks closed by August 1972, the workforce reduced, the salary bill cut and the capital expenditure programme curtailed—produced the following projected results:

1970	Deficit	£2,737,000
1971	Surplus	£ 771,000
1972	Deficit	£1,325,000
1973	Deficit	£1,394,000
1974	Surplus	£ 377,000
1975	Surplus	£ 198,000

These projections were hardly encouraging and the Board's officials continued to press for relief from the interest burden, but the Ministry officials declined to give any assurance on this point.

On the 21st September the Minister himself met the Board's delegation. The Ministry was querying the basis on which the Board could justify continuing to borrow from the Government under the Harbours Act 1964 for the construction of Seaforth Dock whilst discontinuing borrowing from the public on legal advice. (The legal answer would probably be that the Government were being given full financial information which was not available to the public. The political answer, which was no doubt more cogent, was that the Government could hardly be seen to let the port of Liverpool go to the wall.) The Ministry was assured that the completion of Seaforth was essential to the long-term existence of the port and in the event the Government continued to fund the completion by way of 20% port modernisation grants and the balance by Harbours Act loans.

The Minister's position was set forth in a letter to the Board's Chairman dated the 24th September, and the Board's financial crisis received extensive press coverage the following day. On the 28th September the Board issued a press notice in the following terms:

> During recent years The Mersey Docks and Harbour Board have operated under increasingly difficult conditions. The changing pattern of freight movement has tended to move trade away from Liverpool: at the same time labour unrest in the port has not only affected the profitability of the Board but also has lowered the standards of reliability and service which the port has been able to offer to customers. In these conditions the Board have found it difficult to charge their customers rates which could both cover operating expenses and meet interest rates, which have increased partly because of rising market rates on refunded debt and partly because of the interest on new funds raised to modernise the port of Liverpool.
>
> Recently the Board appointed Binder Hamlyn & Co., Chartered Accountants, to make an independent report on the Board's affairs. This report is not yet complete but as a result of preliminary findings by Binder Hamlyn & Co. the Board feel obliged to announce that they face a serious financial situation.
>
> The Board are taking immediate steps to increase their charges, improve their operational efficiency and dispose of surplus assets. In the meantime they will continue to trade and work on the new Seaforth Dock project will be proceeding with the help of loans made by the Minister of Transport under existing agreements as referred to in the attached letter.

In the light of advice tendered to the Board it has been decided that all the Bonds which are due to be repaid on the 27th September, 1970, (including those for which applications for renewal have been received) will be repaid by that date and that any new Bonds subscribed since the 4th September, 1970, will also be repaid together with appropriate interest.

The Board, with the advice of Binder Hamlyn and Co. and Baring Bros. and Co. Ltd. and in close consultation with the Ministry of Transport, are taking all possible steps to evolve, before the end of the year, a plan to ensure the future operation of the port of Liverpool.

A copy of the letter which the Chairman of the Board has received from the Minister of Transport is attached.

The Board appeal to all connected with the port of Liverpool to co-operate to the fullest extent.

Copy of letter from Minister of Transport

Dear Mr. Taylor,

I am writing to let you know the Government's position in relation to the serious financial situation which is the subject of the Board's press announcement today. This letter follows detailed and intensive discussions, during the last few days since this situation became apparent, between your advisers (Binder Hamlyn and Co., Baring Bros. and Co. Ltd., and Slaughter and May) and my officials who have been advised by Mr. John Corbet of Peat, Marwick, Mitchell and Co.

As regards capital works and in particular the Seaforth Dock project the Ministry will continue to make loans in accordance with their existing legal obligations. The position which has arisen is, of course, the responsibility of the Board. The fact that the Government are fulfilling their existing commitments does not imply acceptance of any responsibility for the Board's financial liabilities.

The Government note that the Board are taking immediate steps to increase charges, improve their operational efficiency and dispose of surplus assets. They have been assured that the Board with their advisers are working to produce, as a matter of urgency, a plan to ensure the future viability of the Board's undertaking. All these steps must be pursued with vigour and speed.

My officials will be ready to consider with your advisers any steps which may be proposed from time to time in order to facilitate the development and implementation of the plan referred to. With this in mind, I should be grateful if you would keep me closely in touch with progress.

Yours sincerely
John Peyton

A copy of this notice was sent to all security holders with a covering letter from the Chairman.

Meanwhile, Binder Hamlyn were pursuing their investigation and in an interim report they projected surpluses on the revenue account resulting from the steps taken by the Board to improve their operating finances as follows:

1971	Surplus	£ 619,000
1972	Surplus	£ 221,000
1973	Surplus	£ 242,000
1974	Surplus	£2,116,000
1975	Surplus	£2,643,000

At the same time, cash flow projections showed that large sums of additional finance would still be required largely for the redemption of bonds:

1970	£6,500,000
1971	£6,773,000
1972	£6,883,000
1973	£2,651,000

Binder Hamlyn's conclusion from these projections was that, whilst the revenue account surpluses could not be regarded as satisfactory because they were little more than marginal and were subject to considerable uncertainties, taken at their face value they did not indicate the need or justification for a reduction in the Board's capital debt. However, the situation had to be kept under continuous review and, if the underlying assumptions were not borne out by events, the need for a capital reconstruction might have to be considered.

Binder Hamlyn went on to say that according to the standards by which it had existed in the past, the Board could hardly be judged to be not viable. On the other hand, if the normal commercial standards of the private sector were applied, the Board's revenue account position was far from satisfactory with very little cover for interest payments. The conditions of the past could not be expected to continue indefinitely, but it would take the Board several years to transform its finances into a state which complied with private sector standards of viability. Considerable financial support would be needed in the meantime as it was unlikely that the Board would be able to raise cash from the public after the recent damage to their credit. The only possible source of such support seemed to be the Government.

A copy of this report was sent to the Ministry. Meanwhile, they suggested that the Board should approach the principal holders of bonds falling due in January 1971, a substantial proportion of which were held by large institutions, to seek their agreement to postpone repayment. It was suggested that the Board should also seek assistance from local authorities and shipowners and other port users who had an interest in the port's survival. Soundings in the City of London showed that the financial institutions were not prepared to enter into an unofficial moratorium on their debts. The local authorities were constrained by the limitations on their powers, though they did assist by deferring payment of local rates to the end of their financial year. The port users felt that they were making their contribution by accepting substantially increased charges.

The Secretary of State for the Environment, Mr. Peter Walker, whose Department included the Ministry for Transport Industries, and the Minister held meetings with the top management of some of the major port users, but received a similar response. There was a sharp interchange between the industrialists who had been approached and the Minister. Following their meeting a note was sent by the industrialists' representative stating that in their view the Board and its advisers had not acted irresponsibly in their financial affairs but had been thwarted by the Government and the Bank of England. Likewise there had been continuing interference by the Government to thwart or delay proposed increases in charges. The charges at Liverpool were already higher than at any other major port, and any attempt to pay more of the Board's short-term debt out of revenue by increasing charges would probably have resulted in users transferring business to other ports.

This brought a reply defending the action of the Bank, which in turn provoked an even sharper reply, reiterating the view that the Board's unsatisfactory financial situation was due not, as the Minister alleged, to the incompetence of the Board's management, but rather to the decisions of the previous Government and the Bank of England.

Local Members of Parliament were by now alert to the threat to the Port and lobbied the Minister. In mid-October the senior Conservative statesman, Mr. Selwyn Lloyd, M.P. for Wirral, accompanied by the Board's Director General, had a one-hour meeting. The Director General reported to the Board that he had found the Minister on this occasion more concerned with the humanitarian side of the situation. He was obviously reluctant to see any reduction in the value of the Board's bonds and stock, and he thought that the Minister was keen to avoid a reduction in the capital structure.

Later in October the Minister visited Liverpool and held a series of meetings with interested groups, starting with the Board whom he told that he could give no promise of Government assistance; the Government had set its face against 'bailing out lame ducks'.

He also reiterated his criticism that the voice of port users had counted too much in the past in many ports. The Minister subsequently saw delegations from the Port of Liverpool Staff Association, the Transport and General Workers Union, the local authorities, shipowners and port employers and major port users.

At the beginning of November the Board sent to the Ministry a letter containing an outline plan based on the Binder Hamlyn report covering four areas.

1. Action taken and proposed with a view to the creation of an improved financial position (which had been taken into account in Binder Hamlyn's forecasts).
2. Re-organisation of the management structure: 'We believe the present senior management to be fully capable and certainly to have the necessary experience for carrying out the policies outlined above'. Strengthening of the marketing and financial functions was proposed.
3. Amended constitution of the Board: 'The Board would welcome any suggestion from the Minister in this regard and would appreciate the opportunity of discussing the matter with you'.

4. The need for capital restructuring. The Board pointed out that this would require an Act of Parliament which could not be effective until mid-1971 and that, meanwhile, three tranches of bond would fall due. They suggested that either the Government should guarantee the renewal of these bonds or provide a bridging loan.

The Board saw this letter, with the Binder Hamlyn report, as the plan for which the Ministry had been pressing, or at least as the basis for further discussion. It did not, however, satisfy the Ministry who immediately asked for a more detailed scheme covering, in particular, an amended Board constitution and capital restructuring. As these were matters that could be dealt with only by legislation, it seemed clear that the Ministry's attitude was hardening and that they were likely to force the Board to promote a private Parliamentary Bill to reconstitute itself as a statutory company and to write down its capital. Under the Parliamentary timetable it is necessary for Private Bills to be deposited by the 27th November, and this put great pressure on the Board (who did not, of course, have access to the great resources of expertise available to the Government) to draft a suitable Bill to deal satisfactorily with this complex problem.

At this same time, the Government was grappling with a crisis at the aircraft-engine manufacturers, Rolls-Royce Ltd. On the 11th November, Mr. E. Corfield, the Minister for Aviation Supply, announced in Parliament[1] emergency measures of Government aid amounting to £42 million towards the cost of launching their new RB211–22 engine. This was undoubtedly a considerable embarrassment for the Government,[2] especially for Mr. John Davies, the Secretary of State for Trade and Industry under whom the Aviation Supply Ministry fell, since he had only a week previously made a much publicised speech condemning Labour's financial interventions to help industrial 'lame ducks' and speaking scornfully of 'a soft morass of subsidised incompetence'. The Government's embarrassment was compounded when in January 1971 they had to nationalise Rolls-Royce overnight to save it from total collapse.[3]

There was speculation in the press in November that Mersey Docks were also to be offered assistance. The usually well-informed Michael Baily, shipping correspondent of *The Times*, reported on the 14th November that the Government had offered the Board a loan of

£10 to £20 million to tide them over their immediate financial crisis. 'The conditions are so stringent that the Board were believed to be still considering it last night'. The Ministry were angry about this article and asked the Board's Director General whether any leak had occurred from the Board, and were assured that none had. There is no evidence that any such offer was made and a week later Mr. Baily was reporting that hopes were fading for state help to Mersey Docks.

> The prospect of state financial aid for the port of Liverpool has receded sharply this week amid mounting criticism of the Government's intervention in Rolls-Royce. Refusal of the Government to help the Board after such long discussions would reflect a sudden hardening in Ministerial opinion after widespread charges of inconsistency from people as wide apart as Mr. Harold Wilson and Mr. Enoch Powell. Last week the Board was given to understand that help would be forthcoming subject to certain stringent conditions. But when, after a hectic round of talks, Mr. John Peyton presented his proposals to the Cabinet this week they were turned down flat.
>
> The reason apparently was not that the Mersey Docks and Harbour Board had failed to accept the conditions but that reaction to the Rolls-Royce move had convinced the Government that one 'special case' was in danger of opening the door to a host of others.[4]

The board considered a draft Bill on the 23rd November based on various financial schedules prepared by Barings. After prolonged and agonised discussion, the board authorised the deposit of a Bill which would provide for a moratorium on capital and interest, a write-down of 25% and a new board structure. This Bill, which had been drafted in a great hurry, was intended only as a stop-gap measure, to be replaced in late December or early January by a further Bill to transform the Board to a statutory company, subject to obtaining the necessary Parliamentary approval to the deposit of a late Bill. There was still a belief that the Government would have to offer a bridging loan to cover the bond redemptions due in January (£6.2 million), March (£611,238) and July 1971 (£449,965) since any moratorium under the Board's private legislation could not expect to become effective until July at the earliest, and it would in the meantime be exposed to actions by bondholders, some of them powerful institutions.

The evidence is that the Board's situation was before the Cabinet on the 21st and 28th November and that the decision to reject any request for a bridging loan may have been taken against the recommendation of Mr. Peyton. The reason would seem to have been, as *The Times* speculated,[5] that the Government feared that a second Rolls-Royce would completely undermine confidence in their determination not to 'bail out' sick industries.

To deal with the problem of the bond redemptions due in the first half of 1970, the Ministry suggested that the Government might apply to the High Court on behalf of themselves and all other secured creditors for the appointment of a receiver of the Board's rates. It was hoped that this might achieve a moratorium on redemption until the Board's Bill was enacted. The effectiveness of this move was based on uncertain legal foundations. If a holder of a bond whose redemption was defaulted had made a determined effort to obtain judgement before the Bill was enacted, he might well have been able to levy execution against the Board's assets and thus gain advantage over the holders of securities not due for repayment until after the private legislation had imposed a statutory moratorium, and possibly even cripple the Port.

By now the board members were becoming restive at the Minister's delay in declaring his intentions and at their inability to tell the security holders, port users and employees what was to happen. At a special board meeting on the 26th November it was agreed, after a lengthy review of the situation, not to oppose the appointment of a receiver of rates and to issue a further statement to the press and security holders to coincide with deposit of its Bill. This set out the steps which had been taken and were planned by way of charges increases and revenue savings, the sales of land and control of capital expenditure. The continuing operating losses and the Board's inability to raise further funds in the market meant that 'in the absence of sufficient financial assistance from other sources the Board has no practical alternative but to put forward proposals which will lead to a reorganisation of its capital'. These proposals are summarised below:

1. A two-year postponement of redemption of all securities unredeemed on the date on which the intended Bill was enacted.

2. A reduction in the nominal amount of all securities by up to 30%.
3. The issue of equity shares to security holders.
4. The reconstitution of the Board as a statutory company.

As regards the earlier-maturing bonds, the statement said: 'Meanwhile, ways are being explored of obtaining sufficient finance to meet its commitments, including maturing Bonds, until that time [the passage of the private Bill estimated as not earlier than the end of July 1971]. If sufficient funds cannot be found other action may be taken which could result in Bonds which fall due to be redeemed before any legislation is likely to be passed being included in the proposed capital reorganisation set out above'.

The *Daily Telegraph* of the 27th November contained an authoritative and, as it turned out, a largely accurate account of what the Government had decided to do.

Chapter 5
THE END OF THE BEGINNING

The Government's intentions were finally made known on the 30th November. The Minister summoned the board to the Ministry's bleak office block, St. Christopher House in Southwark. Eleven board members were led by the Deputy Chairman, Sir Joseph Cleary, to whom the Chairman, Mr. Taylor, had to delegate his responsibilities on medical advice.

The Minister told them that their application for a bridging loan or guarantee of their securities from the Government could not be granted, and the Treasury Solicitor would be applying to the High Court for the appointment of a Receiver of Rates. The Government would continue to lend finance for the completion of Seaforth and other approved capital works, and would accept the same write-down of their existing loans as other secured creditors. They wished to see the board appoint a special committee to run their affairs and proposed that Mr. John Cuckney and Sir Matthew Stevenson be co-opted as board members and be made Chairman and Deputy Chairman respectively. Other members of the Committee, he suggested, should be Mr. D. G. Emerson, an existing board member and Chairman of the Mond Division of I.C.I. (who had given approval to his devoting part of his time to the Board's affairs) and Mr. H. Wall, also an existing Government nominated member of the board and local District Secretary of the T.G.W.U. British Rail had given permission for the General Manager of the London Midland Region, Mr. R. L. E. Lawrence, to be available to help the Committee especially on property matters; he became a board member in January, 1971.

Neither Mr. (later Sir) John Cuckney nor Sir Matthew Stevenson was known to board members. Mr. Cuckney was a merchant banker, aged 46, who had recently resigned as a director of Lazard Bros. to become Chairman of the Anglo-Eastern bank. His entry in *Who's*

Who records that after war service he was 'attached to the War Office (Civil Assistant, General Staff)' from 1949–1957, and *Spycatcher* by Mr. Peter Wright, the book which the Thatcher Government tried so hard to suppress, disclosed that, in fact, he worked for British Intelligence.[1] Subsequently, he undertook other tasks on behalf of Government such as Chief Executive of the Property Services Agency, Chairman of the Crown Agents, and Chairman of the Port of London Authority. He has also held many directorships of public companies, including the Chairmanship of Westland Group p.l.c. when it was at the centre of another big controversy of the Thatcher era.

Sir Matthew Stevenson's career was less colourful. He had been a life-long civil servant, retiring earlier in 1970 after four years as Permanent Secretary at the Ministry of Housing and Local Government.

After the Minister had stated the Government's intentions and wishes, the board members questioned him on what would happen if the proposed appointment of a Receiver of Rates failed to achieve the desired comprehensive moratorium, to which the Minister admitted that the situation was fraught with uncertainties, but he believed after discussion with the Solicitor General and other legal advisers that it was the best course available. Members also expressed concern about their responsibility if they delegated powers to an executive committee.

The Minister and his civil servants withdrew and the board resolved to hold a formal meeting, probably the first meeting of the Mersey Docks and Harbour Board outside Liverpool. (Another was held in London in 1971 before the Board was wound up.) The question of their responsibility was discussed and it was agreed that they should meet more frequently than the quarterly meetings that the Minister had suggested.

On the Minister's return he was told that the board agreed to the co-option of Mr. Cuckney and Sir Matthew Stevenson and to elect them as Chairman and Deputy Chairman in place of Mr. Taylor (who had authorised the Director General to tender his resignation) and Sir Joseph Cleary, who also offered to relinquish his position.

Mr. Cuckney and Sir Matthew Stevenson were then introduced to the board and the Chairman designate outlined how he planned his new job, emphasising particularly the need to keep all employees informed of developments. He confirmed that he wished Mr. Edwards to remain as Director General and was delighted to know that he had agreed to do so; this was entirely consistent with the board's view. He also undertook to hold frequent meetings to brief the board.

Following the meeting, the board issued a statement that as the Government would not offer a bridging loan and the Board had not been able to find alternative sources of finance, it would not be possible to pay off the bonds maturing on the 1st January. This was done at the request of the Ministry to establish the basis for an immediate application to the High Court for the appointment of a Receiver of Rates on the grounds that the Board's secured debt was in jeopardy, without waiting for the actual default in January.

Later that day Mr. Peyton made a statement in the House of Commons[2] in which he confirmed that the Government had decided that 'it would be inappropriate and contrary to their general policy to make any contribution towards bridging finance'. He also touched on the Board's deposit of a Private Bill ('as a preliminary measure'), the co-option to the Board of a new Chairman and Deputy Chairman, and the intended application for the appointment of a Receiver of Rates.

The questioning of the Minister on his statement by Merseyside M.P.s exposed the risk that the appointment of a Receiver of Rates would be misunderstood. Mr. Eric Heffer (Walton, Liverpool), for example, described 'the decision to put the port of Liverpool into the hands of the Official Receiver' as 'a scandalous one and an abdication of responsibility by the Government'.[3] Mr. Peyton explained that the Receiver's function would be merely to receive the major part of the Board's income and apply it to meet the expenses necessary for the continued operation of the port; he would have no managerial power.

On the motion of Mr. Heffer, an emergency debate took place the following day.[4] In defending the Government's action, the Minister said:

> [Mr. Heffer] said that the Mersey Docks and Harbour Board did not have the most efficient management in the world. It is essential that the House should be fair to people who have taken part in the management of the Board, a Board which has come in for a great deal of public criticism. I am bound to say that if I were

attempting to set up an organisation to run anything I would not have chosen the Mersey Docks and Harbour Board. But that is in no way to blame the men who took part in it. To have six representatives of shipowners, six representatives of port users aided by four nominees of the Minister, all part time, is hardly a very great recipe for success.

The Hon. Gentleman made his final denunciation of my right hon. and hon. Friends by saying that we were bigoted and dogmatic, and levelled the accusation that we were becoming addicted to this mania or habit of people standing on their own two feet. If that is the gravamen of the Socialist Party's charge against the Government, I am sure that most of us on this side will be very happy to accept it. It seems to us of urgent importance that this country and its immensely significant operations—in which I include the port of Liverpool, of course—should get back to the habit of economic independence and not always be hoping for help, because there will be fewer and fewer in a position to give it.

I believe that one of the troubles here is that Liverpool is almost haunted by the spectre of its past success. There is a great deal too much of the clutter of the past and not only is this physical but it endures in human attitudes as well.[5]

He gave no direct answer to a question from Mr. Eric Ogden (West Derby, Liverpool) about whether the proposals he had put to the Cabinet were 'a good deal more favourable and helpful than the decision he has had to announce today'.[6]

Mr. Joel Barnett, Opposition spokesman on Treasury matters, criticised the proposed write-down of the Board's capital debt which, he said, would have serious implications for many small investors 'who treated an investment in the Mersey Docks and Harbour Board in the same way as they treated an investment in, for example, local government stock'. He appealed to the Minister to reconsider what he described as 'his reorganisation scheme'.[7] The Minister (rather disingenuously) replied: 'It is not my scheme of reconstruction; it is the Board's scheme. Unfortunately, in a hard world, investors who make mistakes are apt to lose their money'.[8]

He rehearsed the four options considered by the Government—to take no action, which would lead only to the 'unthinkable' total closure of the port; secondly, 'equally unacceptable, standing behind the port in all its obligations which would have taught a bad lesson not only to the ports of this country but to every commercial operation which ever looked like running into difficulty'; a bridging operation dealing with a smaller sum of money which would have involved considerable unfairness to some of the bondholders as against others; and the appointment of a Receiver of Rates.[9]

Mr. Selwyn Lloyd defended the Board's position.

> I deprecate this talk about a lame duck. I think that the Board was a lamed duck. It was lamed by the threat of nationalisation and the way in which the previous Government interfered with its borrowing policies. It wanted to borrow £15 million for 10 years and the present crisis would not have arisen if it had been allowed to do it. It was given permission, instead, to borrow only £6 million for 2 years. It has suffered from Government interference and to that extent become a lamed duck. Ideologically, it cannot be wrong to give a crutch to a lamed duck for a time if it will enable it to walk again, and I believe that it could have walked again'.[10]

In winding up the debate, the Secretary of State for the Environment, Mr. Peter Walker, said:

> It has been said that one third of this country is dependent on and related to the activities of this port. With sound management by a new team which includes leading representatives of the trade union movement, I believe, given goodwill, that we shall look back upon this as a tragic incident which brought people to their senses, introduced sound management into a great port and provided a great future for a port which performs such an important activity.[11]

The issue of the write-down was raised again in the House in an adjournment debate on the 18th December,[12] initiated by Mr. Edmund Dell (Labour M.P. for Birkenhead), but supported by a group of Conservative members, Mr. John Tilney (Wavertree, Liverpool), Mr. William Clark (East Surrey) and Mr. Ian Percival (Southport). They criticised the effect that a write-down of fixed interest securities would have on small bondholders and general confidence in the public authority debt market. Mr. Clark, an acknowledged expert on City matters, referred to the Board's bonds as 'a quasi-governmental stock'.[13]

This was an aspect that had been the subject of a powerful first leader in *The Times* of the 4th December:

THE MERSEY DOCKS

Given the City of London's general disposition to favour Conservative Governments and given this Government's particular stress on framing policies to encourage success and to allow business failure it is surprising to see how rapidly relations between the world of finance and government have soured on this issue of public support for failing enterprises. It may be unfortunate for the Government that the first tests of their policy were Rolls-Royce and the Mersey Docks and Harbour Board.

In terms of general philosophy the two may be united. When Mr. Peyton, Minister for Transport Industries, told the House of Commons 'in a hard world investors who make mistakes are apt to lose their money' he would have found many supporters in the financial community. But if he wishes to propound a strict and salutary version of free enterprise it is essential to stick to those rules. And in two fundamental ways the Government seems to have interpreted those rules somewhat oddly.

First there is the contrast between the handling of Rolls-Royce and the Mersey Board. Secondly, the normal method of allowing investors to salvage what they can from their own mistakes is being bypassed as far as the bondholders of the Docks and Harbour Board are concerned.

There would be little serious argument against a Government contention that a general policy of not supporting lame ducks will inevitably allow exceptions—whether those exceptions are based on the defence requirements of the country or the employment needs of particular areas.

But in the light of current policy, where the previous Government could be criticised in making exceptions was in not making investors pay the price for official support. It is hard to see why, for example, under the Labour Government the Cammell Laird Group was given a financial lifeline which allowed its ordinary shareholders to benefit directly and substantially from the injection of public funds. Equally, the present government have saved Rolls-Royce thus protecting the position of the ordinary shareholders, whose shares would have been worth considerably less without public support—while being less than completely candid about the public contribution to this operation [this was a reference to the fact that some of the money given to Rolls-Royce was channelled via the Bank of England, thus minimising the apparent level of Government support].

By the tenets of free enterprise investors in ordinary shares bear the risks and rewards of business. It is unfortunate, therefore, that the first victims of Government policy are investors in fixed interest debentures and bonds in Mersey Docks. And it is doubly unfortunate that a question mark has thus been raised over the security of semi-official borrowings in the bond market.

Even allowing, however, for a rigid interpretation of what is official debt, the pension funds and other investors in Mersey bonds are justifiably incensed at the proposed method of capital reconstruction with which they have been confronted. In a normal commercial enterprise the debenture holders would probably appoint their own receiver and liquidate the assets to cover their securities.

The pension funds would reasonably argue that they are only being prevented from doing so, since the Government oppose the contraction of the port that this would entail. But if Mersey is a special case, the Government should pay the cost of making it an exception. What they cannot do is to confuse the principle of free enterprise with non-commercial practice, particularly at the expense of investors who have chosen safety rather than risk in the placing of their funds.

The Government's application for the appointment of a Receiver of Rates was made in the Chancery Division of the High Court before Goff J. on the 4th December. Leading Counsel for the National Association of Pension Funds and the British Insurers Association applied for a week's adjournment, complaining of lack of consultation. After the week's adjournment, they did not oppose the application and a partner in the leading firm of accountants, Deloittes, was appointed (and continued to act until formally discharged in December 1971).

The board met on the 7th December to make the formal appointment of the new Chairman and Deputy Chairman and to delegate their functions to the Executive Committee. The following were excepted—certain pilotage functions subject to specific statutory provisions; the appointment, dismissal or retirement of principal officers; the election of Board members; and legislation.

Chapter 6
THE EXECUTIVE COMMITTEE

A particular criticism of the Board, especially by the institutional investors—the banks, insurance companies and pension funds—was that there had been no consultation about how the Board should resolve its financial problems. As they saw it, the Board had deposited a Private Bill in Parliament to effect a two-year moratorium and a 30% write-down without any attempt to justify this arbitrary action to those who would be adversely affected. The Board's explanation was, of course, that until the Government gave their answer to the request for financial assistance on the 30th November, the Board was unable to decide how its problems would be resolved and by then, because of the requirements of Parliament's standing orders, a Bill had to be deposited, albeit provisional.

One of Mr. Cuckney's first concerns was to rectify this lack of communication, both with investors and those who worked in the Port. On the 7th December he and the Deputy Chairman met representatives of the National Association of Pension Funds and the British Insurers Association to explain to them the background to the Board's crisis and their preliminary view as to how it should be tackled. As a result of this meeting a Security Holders Committee was set up, comprising representatives of the insurance and pension fund institutions with an appointee of the Public Trustee to represent the interests of the smaller bondholders.

Though many of the institutional investors (particularly those with later-maturing securities) were persuaded to wait at least till the Board's revised proposals were presented, several of the large institutions whose bonds matured on the 1st January 1971 started High Court actions to enforce payment of the bonds. A complicating factor which misled many investors was that the terms of the Board's bonds prescribed by the 1858 Consolidation Act stated that the Board was liable in a penal sum of twice the capital secured if it defaulted on the bond.[1] Accordingly, the writs issued by the plaintiffs in these actions claimed the penal sum or, in the alternative, the capital sum and interest from the date of default. Thus the Hong Kong and Shanghai Banking Corporation and Barclays Bank (London and International) Limited each claimed £2 million by way of penalty or £1 million and interest in the alternative. Samuel Montagu and Co. Ltd. claimed £1,300,000 or £650,000 and interest. The Crown Agents for Overseas Governments and Administrations and their nominee company Four Millbank Nominees claimed £1 million or £500,000 and interest. Various other plaintiffs issued writs for smaller sums.

The Board's defence to these actions was that under a well-established principle of English law the penalty was unenforceable (which was not in the event contested) and that to give judgement on the alternative claims would give those who had sued an unfair advantage over the other and subsequent security holders who ranked *pari passu* in terms of security. These actions were eventually compromised in May 1971 on terms that the Board would submit to judgement for principal and interest lost but the plaintiffs would not enforce the judgements except by joining in the Attorney General's action under which the Receiver of Rates had been appointed, to have his powers extended.

Another matter that engaged the Executive Committee's immediate attention was the Board's capital expenditure plans. Apart from Seaforth, the Board had two other major developments in contemplation, to authorise which it had deposited Bills in Parliament in November 1970. Iron ore for the British Steel Corporation's plant at Shotton on Deeside was imported via Birkenhead docks, but the size of the vessels that could get to the unloading berth at Bidston dock was limited. The Board, in consultation with British Steel, had therefore prepared a scheme for constructing a jetty in the river off Birkenhead docks where much larger vessels could be discharged. Though the scheme was very tentative, the Executive Committee decided to proceed with the Bill; in the event British Steel discontinued steel-making at Shotton and the jetty was never built.

The other Bill was to authorise the siting of a single-buoy mooring off Anglesey for the discharging of crude petroleum to be pumped by a pipe-line to be constructed by Shell to their refinery at Stanlow. This proposed development was also necessitated by the increasing size of vessels which, it was expected, would not be able to get up the River

Mersey to the Board's Tranmere Oil Terminal. The Bill for this had been deposited after only limited consultation with local interests in Anglesey and aroused immediate objections both locally and in Parliament. After a meeting between the Director General and the M.P. for Anglesey, Mr. Cledwyn Hughes, and the Clerk to Anglesey County Council, who both warned of strong opposition to the Board's extending its jurisdiction into Welsh waters, and also because it was thought impolitic to seek powers to borrow some £17 million whilst promoting a Bill to restructure the Board's capital, the Executive Committee decided to drop this project and withdraw the Bill. The mooring buoy was subsequently constructed by Shell themselves and continued to serve their Stanlow refinery until 1988 when crude petroleum imports reverted to Tranmere.

The Executive Committee meanwhile confirmed their confidence in the Seaforth development and at the end of January 1971 the Minister for Transport Industries wrote to say that the Government 'expected' to continue lending capital for this project provided the Board's Bill included provisions ensuring priority for the new loans (including those made since the 27th November 1970) and secured that the capital reorganisation scheme became effective.

By the end of January the revised capital reorganisation proposals had been settled and a long letter, more detailed than any previous circular, had been published.[2] This rehearsed the factors leading to the conclusion that the Board could not continue to support its capital debt—the substantial deficits during the last two-and-a-half years' trading, the expectation of a deficit for 1970 comparable with that for 1969, a decline of some 16% in the net registered tonnage of shipping handled in the Port's docks in the period 1965–1969, obsolescence of dock facilities and the deterioration of labour relations. The Board's proposals were then set out to be incorporated in a Bill to be deposited in place of the original Bill which had been withdrawn on the 21st January. The circular included the warning in heavy type that while the new proposals involved the deferment of a definitive scheme for capital reorganisation until a future date (not later than the 30th June 1974) instead of an immediate write-down of capital by 30% as proposed in the original Bill, the Board had no reason to believe that when put to security holders the definitive scheme would be any less drastic than the original proposals. This circular could not be sent to security holders immediately because of a postal strike, but the

Chairman held a press conference and the contents were widely publicised through the media.

The proposals were given a generally favourable reception as compared with those in the original Bill. Mr. Ken Parry, Chairman of the Investment Protection Committee of the National Association of Pension Funds was quoted as describing them as 'a considerable improvement on those previously placed before Parliament',[3] whilst indicating fundamental differences on one or two points (a reference to the proposed priority for the Government's loans and to the Board's continuing overriding statutory duty to run the Port).

The Chairman also communicated with employees in the Port by the medium of the Board's staff newspaper, the *Port of Liverpool News*,[4] exhorting all to co-operate in regaining for the Port a reputation for **'RELIABILITY'** (emphasised by heavy type as well as capital letters).

Settlement of the 1970 accounts was a major preoccupation of the Executive Committee in the early weeks of 1971. In preparing these accounts the Committee were faced with three particular problems. The value of the Board's land in the 1969 accounts was based on a valuation by the Board's Estate Manager from sales of adjoining and adjacent land. One prospect of a major land disposal had been dashed earlier in December when Oldham Estates finally told the Board they would not be exercising an option to purchase the Albert/Canning areas of the South Docks. Oldham Estates was the company of Harry Hyam, a reclusive but highly successful property developer of the 1960s, to whom the Board had granted an option to purchase this potentially valuable site for £4.3 million at the end of 1966. The firm of Weatherall Green and Smith, who had been retained as property advisers in April 1970, were asked to carry out a comprehensive revaluation of the Board's estate, differentiating between land used for port operations and non-operational land. Weatheralls had tried to find potential buyers for the Board's most prestigious property, its headquarters building at the Pier Head, called by some 'the Dock Office' and by others, more respectfully, 'the Port of Liverpool Building.' Though there was some tentative local authority interest, no firm offers were made. Weatheralls' valuation was not available by the time the 1970 accounts were published and the balance sheet was based on the same value, just over £24 million, as in the 1969 accounts.

The Board's pension arrangements were largely unfunded and paid out of revenue. In January 1971 the Executive Committee engaged consultants to report on the position, but their quantification of the capital cost of the unfunded pension liability and the deficiencies in the funded schemes was also not available for the 1970 accounts, though an estimate of £6.5 million for the unfunded pensions and of £657,000 for the shortfall in the assets of the funds was given in the notes to the accounts.

The third problem was how to calculate depreciation, which had troubled the Board on previous occasions. Here again the Board was still awaiting final advice when the accounts were published, but on the basis of interim advice, taking account in particular of the decision to close the South Docks in 1972, it was decided that £8 million should be written off and deducted from reserves and that an additional £600,000 should be provided for obsolescence.

The deficit shown for 1970 was accordingly £3,028,000, more severe than the 'comparable deficit to that incurred in 1969' (£1,780,000) that had been forecast in the January circular to stockholders.

In his report accompanying the accounts for what he described as a 'troubled and distressing year', Mr. Cuckney said cautiously of the prospects for 1971 'Provided we can keep our costs under control, provided we avoid the damage of self-inflicted wounds, provided we do not drive traffic away by serious and arbitrary interruptions of service, provided we obtain the reliefs sought in the present Bill, we could begin to turn the corner in 1971 and to get out of the red'.

The accounts were issued on the 26th April and for the first time a copy was sent to every security holder.

The Private Bill to give effect to the revised proposals which the Executive Committee had worked out with the Board's advisers and which had been formally approved by the board on the 8th February was deposited in Parliament on Friday the 13th February, permission having been obtained to promote a late Bill. This Bill was 58 clauses and five schedules long, as contrasted with the eight clauses and two schedules of the first Bill. Its main objectives were to transform the Board, the public trust, into a statutory company with a majority of directors elected by holders of the Company's securities. One of the most interesting commentaries on the Bill, in view of his later career, was that of Mr. Nigel Lawson (not yet M.P.) in his financial column in the London *Evening Standard*. The gist of a long article is contained in the following paragraph.

> What Parliament is being presented with is in short a Bill to legalise a major default, coupled with an unashamed element of retrospection. It is a cheap and nasty exercise, which will cause considerable hardship in individual cases, many of which have already come to light. It has also alienated the City which sees it as a blow to confidence in the Government far greater than anything that has occurred over Rolls-Royce.[5]

He concluded: 'The Government should think again—and Parliament should help it to do so'.

A private Parliamentary Bill leading to a private Act differs in essential respects from a public Bill leading to a public general Act. In the words of Erskine May's *Parliamentary Practice*,

> Private legislation is legislation of a special kind for conferring particular powers or benefits on any person or body of persons in excess of or in conflict with the general law. As such it is to be distinguished from public general legislation which is applicable to the general community and is treated in Parliament on an entirely different basis . . . Just as the origin of a private bill, on a petition presented by a person or body outside Parliament, is distinctive, so the proceedings of Parliament in passing these bills differ considerably from the procedure on public bills.
>
> In passing public bills Parliament acts strictly in its legislative capacity; it originates the measures which appear for the general public good, it conducts inquiries when necessary for its own information and enacts laws according to its own wisdom and judgement.
>
> In passing private bills Parliament still exercises its legislative functions, but its proceedings partake also of a judicial character. The persons who are applying for powers or benefits appear as suitors for the bill, while those who apprehend injury are admitted as adverse parties in the suit. Many of the formalities of a court of justice are maintained.
>
> The union of the judicial and legislative functions is not confined to the forms of procedure, but is an important principle in the inquiries and decisions of Parliament upon the merits of private bills. As a court, it inquires into and adjudicates upon the interests of private parties; as a legislature, it is watchful over the interests of the public. The promoters of a bill may prove beyond

> a doubt that their own interests will be advanced by its success and no one may complain of injury or urge any specific objection, yet, if Parliament apprehends that it will be hurtful to the community, it is rejected as if it were a public measure, or qualified by restrictive measures not solicited by the parties.[6]

(A private Bill is not to be confused with a private member's Bill, which is a public Bill that is initiated by a private M.P. as distinct from the Government and, if enacted, it becomes a public general Act.)

The first significant step in the procedure on a private bill is, however, the same as on a public Bill, namely the second reading when the general principles of the Bill are debated on the floor of the House of Commons, in the case of a Bill which starts its progress in the House of Commons (as was the case with the Board's 1971 Bill). The second reading of the Board's Bill took place on the 27th April 1971. Mr. J. M. Temple, M.P. for Chester, who had connections with Liverpool, had agreed to move the second reading on the Board's behalf. In addition to his motion, two instructions had been tabled calling on the committee which would consider the Bill in detail to make specific amendments. Mr. John Tilney, Conservative Member for Liverpool, Wavertree, objected to the proposed repeal of the Board's obligation to maintain the Liverpool ferry landing stage, which was costing the Board some £15,000 per annum to maintain and which consulting engineers had advised would need to be replaced by the end of 1972 at an estimated cost of some £315,000. The day before the debate a provisional agreement had been reached with the local authorities concerned about the future of the Mersey ferry services and this instruction was not pressed.

The other instruction was tabled by Mr. Ian Percival, M.P. for Southport, to the effect that the Bill should be amended to provide that at least half the sum due on redemption of the Board's securities should be paid on the due date or forthwith if already due.

The second reading speeches fell broadly into two categories. The local Members, mainly Labour, were concerned principally about the continuance of the Port. Mr. Edmund Dell, M.P. for Birkenhead, for example, having complained of lack of consultation about the Bill's proposals, said:

> This Bill is not a recipe for removing uncertainty. It is a recipe for three years' continuing uncertainty . . . There is a clear and

> simple way to remove uncertainty. The Government should make a simple statement: 'We will provide for the future of the Port and for its development and for the necessary levels of investment in the Port'. . . The interests of the Port will be sacrificed to the interests of the conscripted loan stockholders. It is entirely wrong that the future of the Port should have to be determined by reference to an uneconomic load of debt.[7]

The Conservative members pressed for some alleviation of the effect on stockholders, especially the small stockholders, as suggested, for example, in Mr. Percival's instruction. This involved them in some difficulty in reconciling their objections with their support for the Government's policy of not subsidising 'lame ducks'. Thus Mr. Percival said:

> Mr. Temple said that the idea was to revitalise the Port. Of course it is, but who should pay? He also said that we must consider the national interest. Of course we must. What I cannot stomach about it all is the apparent readiness of the Board, the Government and some of my colleagues on this side of the House to make the bondholders pay so largely for these things.
>
> I do not believe that the Government's 'lame duck' principle, with which I agree, has anything to do with the case. In fact, Parliament are stepping in here to help the lame duck; the lame duck in this case is the public trust . . . It is helping the lame duck at the expense of the bondholders rather than the taxpayer. We have to ask whether this is something which Parliament should do.[8]

Mr. Tilney departed somewhat from party orthodoxy by suggesting that the Port might be municipalised,[9] and in his speech the Minister for Transport Industries interestingly said 'I certainly have no closed mind on this subject. What would be no solution to the problems of our ports is excessive centralisation. But this is not to say that some degree of municipal ownership or control could not in certain cases be very helpful'.[10] He also appeared to contradict the denials he had made in the previous November that the Board's problems were in any way due to Government or Bank of England constraints. 'During the period of the last Government, and it is time that this was said, and said clearly—the Port's earnings were kept at a meagre level. The Board was obliged to borrow at short term rates, which meant that, if ever there was a moment of truth, there would be trouble'.[11]

The debate ended with a vote for the second reading of 155 to 118.[12] It was notable that, unusually for a private bill, several senior Ministers voted, including the Chancellor of the Exchequer, Mr. Reginald Maudling, and the Minister of State for Trade and Industry, Mr. John Davies, and nine other Cabinet Ministers.

Chapter 7
IN COMMITTEE

The judicial part of the Parliamentary procedure started on the 4th May when the House of Commons Select Committee began consideration of the Bill. The Committee consisted of four Members, two Government back-benchers and two from the Opposition. The Chairman was Mr. (later Sir) Richard Body, trained as a barrister, who had since 1966 represented (and still in 1994 represents) Holland-with-Boston, and Billericay from 1955 to 1959. The other Conservative Member was Mr. Martin Maddan, chairman of a market research company, M.P. for Hitchin from 1955 to 1964 and for Hove from 1965 until his death in 1973. The two Labour Members were Mr. Michael English, M.P. for Nottingham West from 1964 to 1983, formerly an organisation and methods manager, and Mr. Gordon Bagier, M.P. for Sunderland South from 1964 to 1987, a former railwayman.

Petitions against the Bill had been presented by the four bodies who were suing the Board on the defaulted bonds, Barclays Bank (London and International) Ltd., the Crown Agents, the Hong Kong and Shanghai Bank and Samuel Montagu and Co. Ltd. who were jointly represented by Mr. Conrad Dehn Q.C. and Mr. Michael Mann. Individual petitioners appearing in person were Messrs. S. J. Collins, Mr. T. A. Washer and Mr. W. Jacomb, the last named of whom took no active part in the proceedings though he attended the hearing on at least one day. Petitions against detailed provisions of the Bill had also been presented by the British Waterways Board, the Merseyside Passenger Transport Executive and the Birkenhead and Wallasey Corporations, but these were all settled by agreement before or during the course of the Committee proceedings.

The hearings before the Committee lasted eight days spread over the period from the 4th to the 27th May, followed by a ninth day on the 10th June.

On the first morning and early afternoon, the Board's leading Counsel, Mr. Edgar Fay Q.C. (who appeared with Mr. Richard Sykes, a company law specialist)[1] outlined the history of the Bill and took Mr. Cuckney through his evidence-in-chief. The cross-examination by Mr. Dehn commenced that day and continued for the next two days; it was then interrupted for the interpolation of evidence from Mr. Peter Baring and Mr. G. F. Appleton, the Board's auditor, to deal with events before Mr. Cuckney had joined the Board. Mr. Cuckney's cross-examination resumed on the fifth day and he was recalled on the seventh day, after Mr. Edwards had given evidence. These four witnesses were all called by the Board; the petitioners called none.

The evidence ranged widely over the history of the Board's crisis. Counsel for the corporate petitioners sought to show that the Board was not in fact insolvent. This proposition turned mainly on the significance to be given to various land valuations shown in the Board's annual accounts for 1968, 1969 and 1970. In the 1968 balance sheet land was shown as being worth some £5.75 million based on its original cost. However, there was also published a supplementary statement to comply with a request of the National Ports Council to show what the Board's financial position would have been on replacement-cost accountancy principles. In this statement the replacement cost of the Board's land was given as £46 million. The 1969 balance sheet showed land as worth £24 million as at the 31st December, 1969 and explained that the increase as against the figure in the previous year's balance sheet resulted from a revaluation by the Board's Estate Manager derived from the value of land adjoining and adjacent to the Board's estate, an amount equal to the increase having been transferred to general reserve. In the 1970 accounts the same figure, slightly adjusted to take account of small sales and purchases, was used. Mr. Dehn sought, with some initial success, to persuade the Committee that the figure which should have been used in the balance sheet was £46 million, and if this had been done the Board would not have been insolvent.

The issue began to emerge during Mr. Dehn's questioning of Mr. Cuckney on the afternoon of the second day, and at the beginning of the next day's proceedings the Chairman commented:

> The cross-examination reveals assets worth probably another £20 million, and if that is so the Board is solvent or may be, and its

> assets may match its liabilities. In face of that I do not think this Committee can be invited to support legislation which is going to give the Board the privilege—and privilege it is, in the strict legal sense—to say to its creditors 'Well, we are solvent, we can pay our debts, but we are not going to'. That may not be the true situation. We must find out where the truth lies . . . The Board cannot blow hot and cold. It cannot put in the accounts that land is worth £46 million one year and then another year it seems to be £24 million or some other figure. This land is in the heart of a great city like Liverpool and I find it very difficult to believe that land depreciates in value as quickly as that . . . Whether the ferrets in the City have nosed out nuggets of gold or not, I do not know, but certainly we ought to get to the bottom of it.[2]

Mr. Appleton was called to elucidate the position and to say why he had declined to accept the £46 million as a proper figure for inclusion in the balance sheet. He explained that he had insisted that the net book value of docks, quays and river walls should be deducted since the written-down value (some £22 million) would have to be written-off on any disposal of the land.[3] This led into distinctions as to whether a valuation should assume a sale in one piece or in many smaller pieces, and whether on a break-up basis or spread over a longer period to achieve the best prices. In the Board's circumstances the issues seemed rather unrealistic and in the end Mr. Body's 'nuggets of gold' proved illusory.

Depreciation was another accountancy issue which troubled the Committee and Mr. Dehn cross-examined Mr. Appleton at length without being able to get him to agree that the Board had over-provided for depreciation and obsolescence and thus shown a worse position than was justifiable. Mr. Appleton affirmed to Mr. Fay[4] and reiterated to Mr. Dehn[5] that the Board was indeed insolvent. In answer to Mr. Maddan, he said he considered this to be so both on the going-concern basis of being unable to meet its liabilities as they fell due and on the break-up basis, that if the assets of the whole enterprise were sold there would be insufficient to meet the liabilities.[6]

Much cross-examination, including that by Mr. Washer, was directed to whether the Board should have borrowed in 1968, the year when the 1970 maturing bonds were issued, or conversely whether they could in 1970 have again reborrowed to pay off the maturing bonds; in other words, what had happened to make the Board change its long-standing practice? Mr. Baring pointed to 'the cumulative nature of the emergence of a crisis of this type'[7] and Mr. Cuckney said 'Overcapitalisation is like a disease that creeps up on you and unfortunately it is seldom recognised quickly enough'.[8]

The intention of counsel for the institutions in some of his questioning of the Board's witnesses was clearly to induce the Committee to report against the Bill as a whole, to 'find the Preamble not proved' in the Parliamentary terminology, and so throw the problem back at the Government. Thus he asked Mr. Cuckney a series of questions as to why the Bill had been promoted, seeking to adduce that it was done in the national and regional interest. Instead, Mr. Cuckney insisted it had been promoted primarily in the interests of the security holders as a whole. After minute textual analysis of Mr. Cuckney's precise answers, in which the Committee and both Counsel engaged, Mr. Dehn said:

> There is no point in fencing. My position is plain. I thought that this was going to be justified in the national interest and on that basis, in common with most of the Press, the argument I was going to adduce was that if that was so then the expense should be borne by those looking after the national interest and not the bondholders. When I got this unexpected answer I thought it was perhaps a clever but surprising answer, and I pressed it and Mr. Cuckney stuck to it. This was not said to be necessary in the national interest but in the interests of the security holders as a whole.[9]

All the evidence having been heard, Counsel for the corporate petitioners (Mr. Mann, as another commitment had caused Mr. Dehn to be absent) summed up their case.[10] He criticised the Bill as violating two principles, that legislation should not have retrospective effect and that private rights should not be taken away without compensation. The retrospective impact was not only the proposal to nullify any execution to enforce judgement debts on the bonds, but also the cancellation of secured debts incurred before the Bill had even been deposited (unlike the first Bill). After discussion as to whether the Bill was the correct way to resolve the Board's financial difficulties—he declined to concede that the term 'insolvency' was appropriate[11]—he speculated about what would happen if the Bill was not passed.

> We, of course, appreciate that the Government, whilst at one and the same time taking a lively interest in the membership and in particular the chairmanship of the Board, has at the same time said it will not provide any money, and indeed Parliament has been encouraged to pass this Bill. It would be very odd in the circumstances if the Government had done anything else but encourage Parliament to pass this Bill. But what we do not know, of course, is what the Government would do if the Bill was rejected and the national interest was in danger, because hitherto the Government have presumed that this Bill will be approved; it is almost as if Parliamentary approval has been taken for granted . . . If the Bill is not passed, one would obviously wish to inquire, will the Government cease to advance money for Seaforth? And leave £17.5 million worth of half completed docks to be written off? Or will it, on the other hand, notwithstanding the rejection of this Bill, continue to advance the balance of some £16.5 million which is required? We think the most likely course in common sense is that the Government would continue to advance, and that they would not leave £17.5 million worth of half completed docks to be written off, the project being one which has presumably, as an exercise in judgement, been deemed worthy of completion, and been deemed worthy of getting a satisfactory return on the capital invested.[12]

Mr. Mann suggested alternatively that the cost of the Port's continuance should fall on the region rather than on selected creditors.

After Mr. Mann, one of the private petitioners, Mr. Collins, read a prepared statement explaining the hardship which the Board's default had inflicted on him, as a retired person who had invested a large proportion of his life's savings for retirement in a Board bond, a trustee investment. He advocated that the Bill should be withdrawn, all investors be called together to elect a new Board and a fresh start be made.[13]

Mr. Washer, who had earlier played a lively part in the cross-examination of the Board's witnesses but was prevented by illness from attending the later sittings, had prepared a statement which was read to the Committee by his son. He advocated that the Board should be assisted by the Government, the Liverpool Corporation and other corporations in the Mersey area—also the large port users who benefited from improved new facilities.[14]

In answer to the Minister for Transport Industries' statement that the Government believed that to have provided finance 'would have been to put an unjustifiable burden on the taxpayer' Mr. Washer submitted: 'Bondholders are also taxpayers, so this unjustifiable burden is to be borne alone by the tiny proportion of taxpayers whose Bonds fell due for repayment on the 1st January and the 27th March 1971. Is it fair to treat taxpayers so very differently?'[15]

The Committee then retired to discuss their decision and returned later that, the seventh, day. There had obviously been lively debate among the Members. The Chairman admitted that it had not been unanimous in reaching its decision.[16] It subsequently appeared that the Committee had divided two and two, and only the Chairman's casting vote had prevented a report against the Bill.

Mr. English demonstrated his disagreement by withdrawing from the Committee, the Chairman refusing to allow him to explain why publicly; in the event he was present again the next morning.

In declaring the Preamble proved the Chairman made a number of provisoes and asked for 'some radical amendments' [17] to be made. These proposed amendments were the subject of lengthy discussion on the eighth and ninth days.

The first changes which the Committee asked for were limits on the writing-down of the value of the securities, on postponement of redemption and on the reduction in interest. They also wanted the moratorium to end on the 31st December 1972 instead of not later than the 30th June 1974 as in the Bill. Mr. Baring was recalled as a witness on day 8[18] to explain why to impose statutory limitations on these three key elements of the capital reconstruction scheme and to force the new directors to devise their scheme within too short a time would impose an undesirable strait-jacket. The greatest possible flexibility should be allowed to the directors, the majority of whom would be elected by the stockholders, to determine what was best overall for the stockholders in the unforeseeable circumstances obtaining on some future date. Statutory limitations on what they could decide might even, he warned, result in a second insolvency. Mr. Baring's evidence, as the Chairman acknowledged at the beginning of the ninth day,[19] impressed the Committee and they agreed that the directors should be unfettered in discharging their general duty 'to provide for such minimum alteration of the rights, privileges, restrictions and obligations attaching to the new securities . . . as shall, having regard to the financial position of the Company, at the time the scheme is prepared, be necessary to secure, so far as practicable, the financial viability of the Company' (s.48(1)(a) of the 1971 Act). As Mr. Maddan put it in the subsequent debate on the floor of the House of Commons:

> Mr. Baring made it clear that there were three factors, all of which were interdependent. There was the amount of the write-down, the amount of interest payable, and the length of postponement of the redemption of the debt. It is like a bath with three plug holes. Unless all three are stopped up, one might as well not stop any one at all because in the end all the water can escape.[20]

The date by which the scheme was to be submitted to separate meetings of the four categories of security holders—bondholders, debenture stockholders, annuity holders and the Government—was, after further discussion, settled at the 30th June 1973.

The Bill proposed that if the directors' scheme was not approved by the stipulated majority in number representing 75% in value of the investment at all the meetings, the scheme should be referred for final settlement to an independent expert to be appointed by the President of the Institute of Chartered Accountants. This had been criticised and the Board had offered to amend the Bill to provide for appeal to a panel of three experts. The Committee, however, insisted that any appeal should be to the High Court, but that to avoid any undue delay the Court should be required 'so far as practicable' to approve the scheme before the 31st December 1973 and that the decision of the court of first instance should be final.

The issue of depreciation continued to concern the Committee and they asked the Board to give an assurance that depreciation would continue to be charged during the moratorium period on a straight line basis on historic costs over the estimated lives of the assets as in the 1969 and 1970 accounts, and not on replacement costs, subject to the ongoing review of asset lives.

The Chairman acknowledged the influence that Mr. Collins' submissions had on the Committee's thinking,[21] and to mitigate the hardship resulting from the moratorium on the bondholders most harshly affected, the Board agreed at the Committee's insistence to provide for the payment of half, up to a maximum of £500, of the sum due on a bond maturing in the moratorium period to any bondholders entitled to claim small-income relief under income tax law.

Finally, of their own motion, the Committee insisted that the Bill should limit the inclusion on the new board of directors of members of the former board. Remarks from the Chairman and Mr. English made clear the Committee's opinion that former board members bore a considerable share of blame for the insolvency. For example, the Chairman, in stating the Committee's preliminary decision on day seven, said 'the dividing line between culpability and criminality can be very slender, and one wonders on which side the Board has been in the past over some matters'.[22] Consequently, there was inserted in the provisions relating to appointment and election of directors a restriction that during the moratorium period no person (except the persons specifically named in the Bill as the first directors) should be eligible to become a director if he was a director of any body corporate at the time when in respect of any part of its income or assets a receiver was appointed or which was wound up compulsorily, except with the approval of the Secretary of State.

The Committee insisted on the inclusion in the Company's interim constitution of a requirement that the directors elected by the security holders (not less than four nor more than five) and appointed by the Minister (not more than three) should, in exercising their power to co-opt up to four more directors, ensure that at least one was appointed after consultation with the trade unions recognised for negotiating purposes by the Company.

The Bill returned to the floor of the House of Commons on the 21st June for consideration of the Bill as amended. On the general principle there was little new to be said, though that did not inhibit Members during a four-and-a-half-hour debate from rehearsing the arguments as to whether or not the Government should have assisted the Board and left them to promote a Bill which all Members found distasteful. Several Members on both sides were critical of the comments made by the Committee about the culpability of former board members, since none of the people embraced by this blanket condemnation had been heard in his own defence. Mr. Tilney read from a letter which he had received from Mr. Morton Oliphant, Chairman of the Board from 1964 to June 1969; other Members pointed out that his successor, Mr. Taylor, had died in April 1970.[23]

At the end of the debate Mr. English, supported by other Members, queried whether the statutory duty in the Bill as drafted sufficiently guaranteed the continuation of the Port of Liverpool, and it was agreed by the Minister and Mr. Temple on behalf of the promoters that this should be given further consideration.[24] This issue also concerned Liverpool Corporation, who at a special meeting later that month resolved to oppose the Bill in the House of Lords unless they could be satisfied as to the new Company's statutory duty. In the short third reading debate on the 1st July, the Solicitor General, Sir Geoffrey Howe, gave an assurance that as a statutory company with statutory duties, the Company could not be relieved of these duties, even in a liquidation, without Parliament's approval in the form of another Bill.[25] On this basis, the Bill was given an unopposed third reading and the Corporation of Liverpool withdrew their opposition. After a forty-minute debate in the House of Lords on the 13th July[26] and other formalities, the Bill received the Royal Assent on the 27th July, 1971 and came into operation on the 1st August.

The old board met for the last time on the 30th July 1971, when 12 members were present.

The last meeting of the Mersey Docks and Harbour Board on the 30th July 1971. From left to right: Mr. R. E. Lawrence; Mr. D. G. Emerson; Mr. J. D. Wilson; Mr. J. H. Wall; Sir Matthew Stevenson (Deputy Chairman); Mr. R. S. F. Edwards (Director General); Mr. J. G. Cuckney (Chairman); Mr A. Lynch (Secretary); The Earl of Carrick; Mr. P. G. Clarke; Sir Joseph Cleary; Mr. W. B. Briscoe; Mr. N. M. Bacon; Mr. M. A. Nicolson (photograph courtesy of the *Liverpool Daily Post and Echo*)

Chapter 8
BUSINESS AS USUAL

Despite the amount of time that the Chairman and Director General in particular had to devote to the Parliamentary proceedings, the Executive Committee continued to meet weekly throughout the first seven months of 1971. Apart from resolving problems relating to the 1970 accounts as already described, they were also concerned with reorganising the management structure with a view particularly to strengthening the financial and marketing functions. To this end, in March Mr. H. G. Wrigglesworth, a Chartered Accountant, was recruited from outside as Director of Finance with the responsibilities of devising, installing and operating procedures for the effective financial management of the affairs of the Board, and from within Mr. G. W. Brimyard was appointed Director of Operations and Marketing and Mr. J. B. Fitzpatrick Director of Personnel and Industrial Relations. At this stage none had the status of Board director.

By June the financial estimates of the eventual cost of Seaforth were escalating towards £50 million and the Chairman asked for a short paper to answer the questions 'Is it worth it?' and 'Is it a good idea?' The Department of the Environment, who were financing the project, were also concerned. Meanwhile, however, construction was proceeding and on the 5th July the flooding of the new dock started without any formal ceremony. Later that month the Minister for Transport Industries announced that the payment of port modernisation grants under the Harbours Act 1964 was to be discontinued. He excepted, however, grants in respect of 'contracts still to be let as an integral part of the present Seaforth dock scheme on the Mersey'.[1]

The members of the first Board of directors of the new Company to serve until a general meeting could constitute a new Board were named in the Act and were in fact the members of the Executive Committee, with one important exception. At the end of June the Board had announced the retirement, with effect from 31 July, of Mr. Edwards, the Director General. He had been told by the Minister on the eve of the passing of the Bill that he was not to be named in the Bill as one of the first directors of the Company, as had been the intention—at least ostensibly—up to that point. A last-minute change to the Bill substituted for the name of Mr. Edwards as a first director of the Company that of Mr. G. W. Brimyard, who had been promoted to Managing Director. Mr. Cuckney said: 'I particularly wish to record how much I enjoyed working with the Director General and how valuable his support and assistance have been during a very critical period. The Port of Liverpool undoubtedly owes a lot to Mr. Edwards'.[2] This was a sentiment widely felt on Merseyside, on whose behalf Mr. Edwards had (as Sir Joseph Cleary put it, as reported in the *Daily Telegraph*) suffered 'a very rough, tiring and trying time.'[3]

At the first meeting of the new Board on the 2nd August 1971, Mr. Wrigglesworth and Mr. Fitzpatrick were co-opted as board directors. Mr. Cuckney summarised what he saw as the major problems to be tackled.

1. Complete re-appraisal of the financial situation and prospects and commitments.
2. Disposal of surplus properties and assets.
3. Full explanation of the escalating costs of Seaforth.
4. Cargo handling—to decide in the light of the profitability of the operation whether to remain in cargo-handling and the labour and policy implications.
5. The image of the new Company—the need to put over to the public and commercial interests the right image and to improve the Company's reputation.

The Liverpool Corporation had decided that they did not wish to acquire the Dock Office for their own occupation. There was a possibility of the planned Merseyside local authority's purchasing it as their headquarters, but this would not be established before 1974. In the meantime, it was agreed that the Company's occupation of the building should be contracted to release space for sub-letting.

The cargo-handling operations were losing £.25 million a year which, it was realised, the directors soon to be elected by the stockholders would find unacceptable unless either there was a real prospect of their becoming profitable or their being justified as a marginal loss operation for the good of the Company's overall business.

The Company's first general meeting was held on the 3rd November. Liverpool's Philharmonic Hall had been booked, with a capacity of some 2,000. In the event only about 150 stockholders attended. The formal business of the meeting was to elect five 'B' directors. Before proceeding to the election, the Chairman made a short statement giving a guardedly optimistic forecast of the financial results for 1971, but warning that 1972 was going to be a difficult year with Seaforth 'coming on stream but not fully earning its keep'.

There followed a short session of questions to the Chairman, some of a technical nature, such as the capacity of the Gladstone river entrance to cope with the Seaforth traffic, some of a candle-end nature, but mostly about the prospects of stockholders recovering their investments in full. One question that might have been asked but was not, was whether in light of the trading profit actually achieved in 1971 the Board could properly in 1970 have continued its usual practice of reborrowing to redeem maturing bonds.

The meeting then proceeded to the only formal business of voting on the election on the five candidates nominated by the existing board for election as 'B' directors. There had been only two other valid nominations for election as 'B' directors, one an official of the Amalgamated Engineering Union and the other described as Chairman of the Association of Gilt-Edged Security Holders Limited. In fact the Company Chairman held proxies which would enable him to ensure that the official candidates were elected, but on a show of hands at the meeting the two unofficial nominees were voted down.

The five 'B' directors were accordingly Mr. J. P. Bingham, a Liverpool stockbroker, Mr. E. J. Guthrie, general manager of the Liverpool-based Royal Insurance, Mr. Geoffrey Heywood, senior partner of a leading firm of actuaries, Mr. G. L. Tillotson, recently retired as chairman of his family firm of printers and board-makers and involved in many Liverpool activities, and Mr. J. V. Woollam, a merchant banker who had been M.P. for the Liverpool, West Derby constituency from 1954 to 1964. Additionally, the Secretary of State for the Environment had given official notice of appointment as 'A' directors of Mr. Cuckney, Mr. Emerson (who replaced Sir Matthew Stevenson as Deputy Chairman) and Mr. P. J. Butler, a partner in Peat Marwick and Co., Chartered Accountants.

The 'A' and 'B' directors at their first meeting appointed as 'C' directors, Mr. Wall, as a non-executive director, and Messrs. Brimyard, Fitzpatrick and Wrigglesworth, making a board of 12 directors in all.

On the 6th December the Blue Star Line vessel *Tasmania Star* carrying meat from New Zealand, was the first ship to enter Seaforth Dock for discharge at the new meat berth. Mr. Peyton visited the Port for the occasion.[4]

As predicted by the Chairman at the general meeting, the Company's first annual accounts recorded a far healthier year's trading than the Board's final accounts. The 1970 loss of just over £3 million had been turned round to a profit of £1.575 million, even after extra provisions for pension liabilities. This was acknowledged to be due mainly to the increases in charges aggregating nearly 45% made in 1970 and early 1971, resulting in an increase in revenue of about £4.8 million. Out of this profit, the Company was able to pay the interest withheld from payments made between the date the Act became effective and the end of the year, amounting to £261,000 (including £76,500 payable to the Department of the Environment).

Though depreciation was charged in the profit and loss account on the same basis as in the 1970 accounts, by the straight line method from historical cost, in accordance with the undertaking given to the House of Commons Select Committee, extra provision for depreciation and obsolescence of a further £1.6 million was written off against reserves as a result of the review of asset lives that had been referred to in the 1970 accounts and before the Select Committee.

Additionally, a detailed inventory of assets disclosed that assets with a book value of £921,000 no longer existed or had been abandoned (such as railway lines that had been taken up, abortive dredging and abandoned jetties at Dingle and obsolete graving dock machinery). This sum also was written off against reserves. Finally the independent valuation of the Company's land (other than newly created land at Seaforth) referred to in the 1970 accounts resulted in a figure of about £24 million, a reduction from the previous valuation of about £4.2 million. No doubt to avoid any risk of repetition of the confusion that had arisen from the various land valuations in the 1969 and 1970 accounts, the directors had Weatherall's valuation examined and agreed by local valuers, Edmund Kirby and Sons, and a painstaking note was included in the accounts setting out in detail the assumptions underlying the valuation.

The effect of these various adjustments to the balance sheet, even after the year's retained profit and certain other sums had been credited, was to leave a deficit on general reserve of £2.2 million.

The statement accompanying the 1971 accounts was Mr. Cuckney's last. As he had told the board on the 7th February he would, he retired from the board of directors on the 26th April 1972, for business and health reasons. His resignation had been preceded on the 1st April by that of the deputy chairman, Mr. Emerson. Their successors were Mr. Guthrie, as deputy chairman, and Mr. (later Sir) J. J. Page as chairman. Mr. Page (57) after war service in the R.A.F. (rising to the rank of Group Captain) had been employed until 1970 by the Iraq Petroleum Company.

Sir John Cuckney: Chairman of the Board, 1970–72

Chapter 9
ANNUS HORRIBILIS

As Mr. Cuckney had predicted in his statement accompanying the 1971 accounts and repeated at the annual general meeting in April, 1972 was to be a difficult year, though he could hardly have foreseen the sequence of setbacks that were to occur in the year which was intended to establish the financial platform upon which the capital reconstruction scheme was to be based. A harbinger for the new Chairman, Mr. Page, was that on the day he chaired his first board meeting the dockers held a day's strike for a May Day rally.

The year's problems originated predominantly from industrial disputes. Turmoil was endemic in the docks industry, not just in Liverpool, during most of 1972, originating in the spread of containerisation and focused principally on a struggle between the Transport and General Workers' Union and the National Industrial Relations Court. The Court had been established under the Industrial Relations Act, passed in 1971 with the object of imposing a stricter legal framework on industrial relations. The T.U.C. had decreed a boycott of the Act and its institutions. In March 1972 the St. Helens road hauliers Heatons were granted by the National Industrial Relations Court an order restraining the T.G.W.U. from blacking imposed by Liverpool dockers on containers carried by Heatons' lorries, on the grounds that by stuffing and stripping (i.e. packing and unpacking) these containers at their own premises Heatons were depriving the dockers of work which they contended should be done by them. The T.G.W.U., in accordance with T.U.C. policy, were not represented at the Court hearing and ignored the order. The Court then imposed a fine on the Union of £5,000 and gave them three weeks to pay on pain of sequestration of their assets. This too the Union ignored, as well as orders against blacking made by the Court on the application of other hauliers. This led in April to the imposition of a fine of £50,000 for contempt of court. On the advice of the T.U.C. the Union paid the fines, but the blacking continued in Liverpool.

As Mr. Lew Lloyd, the local T.G.W.U. official, explained, 'I don't agree with the decision [to continue the blacking]. I advised that they should not black the job against the law but the dockers feel they are not breaking the law because their Union does not accept the Industrial Relations Act'.[1] The Liverpool dockers even turned down a personal appeal by the Union's General Secretary, Mr. Jack Jones, a former docker himself at neighbouring Garston docks.[2]

On the 5th May a docks delegate conference of the T.G.W.U. called for a national docks strike to back claims for improved holiday and fall-back pay, but agreed to postpone the strike on the setting up of a committee jointly chaired by Lord Aldington, Chairman of the Port of London Authority, and Mr. Jones and comprising port chairmen and senior union officials, with wide, if imprecise, terms of reference to consider what were described as 'the problems confronting the ports industry'.

On the 13th June the Court of Appeal set aside the fine against the Union on the grounds that the Union could not be held responsible for the actions of the shop stewards who were organising the blacking. The previous day, however, an unofficial committee of shop-stewards of London dockers had been ordered by the National Industrial Relations Court to stop picketing a container depot at Stratford, East London and, when they disregarded the order, three shop stewards were committed to prison. This order was quickly challenged in the Court of Appeal by a court official whose existence until then had been largely unknown, the Official Solicitor (whose functions related mainly to safeguarding the interests of children and the mentally ill), acting without the knowledge of the three stewards, and the Court revoked the imprisonment order. On the 21st July five more London dockers were imprisoned for contempt of court for disregarding an order not to picket a cold store in Stratford, precipitating an immediate stoppage in London, Hull and Liverpool docks as well as widespread protests and stoppages in other industries. This time there was no appeal against the imprisonments, but on the 24th July the National Industrial Relations Court itself ordered the dockers' release on the grounds that the House of Lords had just ruled on appeal in the Heaton case that, contrary to the judgement of the Court of Appeal, a union was responsible for the actions of its shop stewards taken in pursuance of union policy, and thereby made it clear that the primary method of enforcement contemplated by the Industrial Relations Act was against union funds rather than individuals. This averted an almost certain national strike not just of dockers, but of many other groups of workers such as miners, railwaymen and printers.

On the 25th July the Aldington-Jones Committee rushed out an interim report in the hope of averting the national dock strike called for by the docks delegate conference in May. The report recommended that all dockers on the National Dock Labour Board's temporarily unattached register should be allocated to full-time employment with a registered employer by the 4th September; an improvement in voluntary severance terms for a limited period to be offered to medically unfit men and those over 55; and that unions, port authorities and employers should seek agreements with outside interests 'to establish to mutual advantage clear lines on which container groupage should be performed in future without disturbance'. This was accompanied by a Government announcement that for five months it would meet the full cost of severance payments to dockers over 55 and medically unfit.[3]

The recalled docks delegate conference meeting on the 27th July, however, rejected the Committee's recommendations and, by a majority of 38 to 28 with 18 abstentions, resolved to go ahead immediately with a national strike. This was a clear snub to Mr. Jones and the other union officials (including Mr. Lloyd from Liverpool) who had put their names to the Report. The Committee went back into session and, largely by the efforts of some port chairmen, managed to obtain promises of a few extra jobs for dockers in transport depots and cold stores close to dock estates. Another docks delegate conference meeting on the 16th August agreed to call off the strike by 53 to 30 but the shop stewards in major ports, including Liverpool, decided to continue the strike unofficially. A mass meeting of 5,000 Liverpool dockers (out of about 10,500) on the 18th August unanimously voted to continue the strike, Mr. Lloyd not being allowed to address the meeting. In other ports, however, the return to work decision was honoured and, when the Liverpool men heard that the London and Hull dockers had voted to return to work despite their shop stewards' recommendation to stay out, a further mass meeting only three days later voted 'by an overwhelming majority' for a resumption 'in view of the national situation'. The Liverpool dockers had been on strike for about three weeks.

While all this activity (or, frequently, inactivity) was going on at the national level, major problems relating specifically to Liverpool had blown up. The first container berths at Seaforth were due to become operational on the 10th May and the container facilities as a whole were scheduled to be ready by October. The Company believed that agreement had been reached with the T.G.W.U. in 1971 on the terms of employment of registered dock workers at the container berths, but the port shop stewards took advantage of the opportunity to refuse to allow the opening of the berths unless the 35–hour week agreed for Seaforth was conceded throughout the Port. This was in fact conceded in principle, but negotiations on the detailed implementation were frustrated by the Government wage freeze in November.

In June three of the private stevedoring companies in the Port, A. E. Smith Coggins Limited, Port of Liverpool Stevedoring Company Limited and Ocean Port Services Limited, announced their intention to close their Liverpool operations. As between them these companies employed nearly half the registered dock workers in the Port, this represented a major crisis for the Company as port authority. To allow them to go into liquidation without any provision for taking over their activities would cause major disruption both in industrial relations and to the Port's trade. On the other hand, it was obviously most unpalatable for the directors of the Company, especially those elected by the stockholders, to be forced to take over loss-making businesses within a year before having to submit a capital reconstruction scheme to those stockholders. The most urgent case was that of Smith Coggins. Whereas the other two stevedoring companies were subsidiaries of shipowning businesses (Clan Line and Furness Withy in the case of Port of Liverpool Stevedoring and Ocean Fleets in the case of Ocean Port Services), Smith Coggins were an independent company with no parent company to back them and they seemed likely to go into liquidation within weeks. Talks between them and the Company started immediately. The dockers' jobs were effectively secured under the terms of the Dock Labour Scheme and the Aldington-Jones recommendations, though reallocating them between the remaining employers was only likely to destabilise their positions. The position of the supervisory and clerical workers was not assured and 800 of this group who were members of the

Association of Clerical Technical and Supervisory Staff, a section of the T.G.W.U., struck in support of a claim to be taken onto the National Dock Labour Board register in order to obtain similar job security and redundancy payments as registered dock workers. A further complication was that the employees of the Company's own engineering department, who were resentful that fitters employed to maintain cargo-handling plant were paid a substantially higher wage than general fitters, objected to the Company's taking on fitters from other companies to be paid at the higher rate.

Though in the circular[4] sent to stockholders to justify what were termed the cargo handling 'mergers' the Company emphasised the positive aspects such as the scope for rationalisation of administrative and financial control and the economies of scale, this could best be described as making a virtue out of necessity, and these mergers came at a most inopportune time, and at least in the short term were clearly going to impose considerable burdens on the Company's finances. Application was made to the Government for financial assistance to purchase plant and equipment, for the provision of working capital and subsidisation of the expected losses while the merged operations were rationalised. This application, which had to be considered by two Government departments, Transport and Trade and Industry, was still under consideration when Smith Coggins announced that they would be ceasing business on the 17th September and the local Dock Labour Board allocated their registered dock workers to the Company. The directors held a special meeting on the 11th September. Though aware of the dilemma facing the Company, the four 'B' directors present could not bring themselves to vote for the merger without having any assurance of satisfactory Government assistance and abstained on the formal vote, which was accordingly carried by seven votes to nil. The Company took over Smith Coggins' operations on the 17th September. Talks were continuing with the other two stevedores. A principal concern of the Company in these negotiations was to secure some guarantee from the parent companies that they would continue to use the Port, which Ocean Fleets in particular were reluctant to give for reasons which became clear when they transferred their important Far East traffic to Southampton. Eventually the acquisition of these two businesses was completed in February 1973. The Government's decision on the application for financial assistance was received in December 1972, when the

Department for Transport Industries offered a loan not exceeding £617,000 for the acquisition of assets, and the Department of Trade and Industry a loan not exceeding £1.75 million for working capital and a grant not exceeding £1.75 million to cover any losses on the merged cargo-handling operations up to the 30th June, 1973 under the recently enacted Industry Act 1972. Directors were concerned at this cut-off date for loss subsidisation, but it was agreed to accept the offer and pursue negotiations with the Department of Trade and Industry for assistance towards any post-June losses.

The national dock strike had postponed the closure of the South docks, originally scheduled for the end of August 1972, until the 29th September. The completion of Seaforth was seriously delayed by a prolonged national strike in the construction industry in August and September. Even when the Grain Terminal was handed over to the Company, a dispute between the docks section of the T.G.W.U. representing registered dock workers and the the Association of Clerical, Technical and Supervisory Staff about who should man the control centre at the Terminal prevented its commissioning during 1972 and indeed throughout 1973 and until the autumn of 1974.

The Company's half yearly report was sent to stock-holders on the 28th September, showing a profit for the period to the 2nd July of £178,000 net of redundancy costs, depreciation and interest (at the reduced 70% rate). This profit, small as it was on a revenue of nearly £12.5 million, was, however, to be overwhelmed by the loss in the rest of the year. Even before the interim report had been sent out, the Finance Director was giving the Board an estimate for full year of a £2 million loss as a result principally of the national dock strike which had cost the Company some £1.6 million, reduction in revenue because of a decline in traffic of £300,000, delays at Seaforth costing £250,000 and an additional £400,000 for redundancy payments.

The outlook was so bleak that the directors discussed the possibility of seeking to postpone the capital reconstruction scheme even though this would require another Parliamentary Bill, thus reopening the whole controversy. Advice was also taken on whether the Company could submit an interim scheme by the statutory deadline which postponed the final scheme to a later date, but Counsel advised that this could be challenged as not complying with the Act. The Security Holders Committee had been kept informed about the Company's problems and favoured a postponement. They had approached the

Ministry for Transport Industries about the possibility of assistance under the Industry Act 1972 to ameliorate the scheme, but were given no encouragement.

Though charges were kept under review, it was felt—having regard to the disruption in the service offered by reason of the strikes, aggravated towards the end of the year by a shortage of dock labour as a result of 2,600 registered dock workers having taken advantage of the new redundancy scheme to leave the industry—that the Company's competitive position would be seriously damaged by another general increase in the Port's main charges. In September the Liverpool Master Porters Association, representing all cargo-handling operators (including the Company, the largest master porter in the Port), asked the Company to promote a bye-law to increase charges for master porterage (i.e. charges made to importers for off-loading goods from quays and transit sheds). This application was supported by an independent financial assessment quantifying the increase in the master porters' costs resulting largely from the Aldington-Jones recommendations. However, when the Company submitted a bye-law to the Ministry for Transport Industries in November for approval, it was asked not to proceed in view of the Government's policy of price restraint as set out in the White Paper *A Programme for Controlling Inflation: The First Stage*.[5] Whether or not history ever truly repeats itself, this situation bore a disconcerting similarity to events which had contributed to the Board's insolvency. No increase in the Company's general charges was made until the spring of 1973, after the relaxation of the Government's counter-inflationary policy.

The decision whether to deposit a Bill to defer the capital reconstruction scheme was postponed until almost the deadline of the end of November set by the Parliamentary timetable, but then it was agreed by the directors to be pointless as financial forecasts predicted continuing financial problems as far ahead as 1977.

The loss for 1972 as reported in the annual accounts published in mid-April 1973, only two-and-a-half months before the deadline for the submission of the capital reconstruction scheme to stockholders, was £1,763,000.

Sir John Page: Chairman of the Company, 1972–77 and 1980–84

Chapter 10
THE SCHEME: PHASE ONE

Preliminary consideration of the terms of the capital reconstruction scheme had started towards the end of 1971. The turbulent events of 1972 made financial forecasting extremely difficult so that it was impossible to formulate any firm conclusions as to the overall severity of the scheme until much nearer the date for its submission. However, two aspects of the scheme could usefully be discussed, namely the scope or general shape of the scheme (i.e. the relationship between the reduction in the nominal values of the fixed-interest securities and the length of deferment of redemption dates, and whether and to what extent an equity element should be introduced into the Company's capital structure), and the method of allocating the new securities. Barings submitted a paper in November 1971 outlining preliminary suggestions on these aspects. As regards the scope, they pointed out that the choice the directors would have to make would be between minimising the write-down in recognition of the fact that the investors had chosen to invest in fixed-interest securities and not in equities, and a drastic write-down to ensure so far as possible the Company's future viability offset by the issue of shares with the prospect in time of compensating the investors for their losses by payment of share dividends.

The method of allocation of the new stock and shares, if any, to be issued under the scheme was bound to be complicated since it had to ensure as far as possible that the holders of 70 redeemable securities, with a wide variety of redemption dates and interest rates, and 12 varied irredeemable securities should have the same proportionate interest in the Company by virtue of the newly issued securities, taking account of the differential effect of the postponement of maturities and also, as the Act required, the effect of early part redemption payments made under the small-income relief provision of the Act. Barings calculated some complex actuarial formulae to this end based on the pre-scheme value of the securities as at the 1st January 1971, the first date on which alteration of the rights in the Board's securities began *de facto*, and estimated, in the absence of market prices, on a yield curve derived from widely traded local authority fixed-interest stocks. This method of allocation, though initially criticised by some as unduly complicated, withstood the scrutiny of experts advising the insurance companies and other institutional investors and, eventually, of the High Court assessors to form the essential basis of allocation made under the eventual scheme.

The Finance Director continued throughout 1972 to revise and update the five-year revenue and cash-flow forecasts as best he could in all the circumstances and to go over them with the Company's financial advisers and the Finance Committee of the Board of directors. Among factors which had to be determined before a scheme could be settled were two which involved prolonged negotiations with Government departments. Cash-flow forecasts depended on the extent to which the Company had to finance capital expenditure or, alternatively, could rely on the Government's continuing financial support, there being no prospect of any other source of borrowing within the time-scale covered by the forecasts. A matter which was of particular concern to the Security Holders Committee was whether the Government would agree to give up the priority on their post-27th November 1971 loans so as to rank *pari passu* with other post-scheme stock. The Government made it clear that this would depend on whether they were satisfied that the scheme secured the Company's future viability. (There was a hope in some quarters that the Government would agree to their priority loans being written down in line with all the other securities, including their own non-priority loans, but it had been made clear during the debate on the Bill that they had no such intention.) The cargo-handling mergers introduced another factor requiring decisions from Government, as already described, namely the extent of subsidy especially for any continuing losses.

At first sight the closure of the South Docks appeared to offer the Company an opportunity to realise a valuable asset and thus enable it to devise a less severe scheme. Discussions were held with the Liverpool Corporation as planning authority about what uses a developer would be permitted to make of the 300-acre site. The local authority were themselves a potential purchaser but they could only afford such a major acquisition if they could be assured of getting an 85% dereliction grant from central Government; to categorise the site as derelict land would, however, severely depress the price that the Company could expect to receive. Moreover, the Corporation proposed to fill the docks with household refuse which would have delayed building on the site for decades unless special piling was used, whereas the Company advocated filling hydraulically with sand pumped from the estuary to allow quicker development.

Mr. Arthur Dooley,[1] the Liverpool sculptor, founded a company, the South Docks Development Company, which commissioned a feasibility study to assess the possibility of developing the 300 acres for residential, industrial and recreational uses. He planned to involve trade unions, tenants' associations and similar groups who, he hoped, would take shares in the Company. Surprisingly, his initial plan envisaged clearance of the Albert Dock with its grade 1 listed dock warehouses for housing.

During 1972 schemes for development of two particular parts of the area were under discussion. The Canning Dock site was being considered for the erection of Government offices and, if these plans had come to fruition, it could have primed the acquisition of a much larger area, perhaps the whole of the South Docks, by Heron Corporation, who were negotiating to build the Government offices. The Albert Dock area was under consideration as the possible site for relocating the Liverpool Polytechnic,[2] whose facilities were widely scattered round the city.

In the event, neither of these schemes came to fruition and discussions with various interests about disposal of the South Docks in whole or part dragged on into 1973, beyond the time when any proceeds of sale could be assumed in devising the scheme.

Towards the end of 1972 the Security Holders Committee proposed an alternative scheme basis designed to preserve an eventual right to the money lost by stockholders. Those whose capital was not repaid in full on the postponed dates prescribed by the scheme or whose income entitlement was reduced would on each occasion receive a certificate. The Company would be required to set up a surplus fund into which it would pay all profits after an agreed depreciation provision, say £3 million, and from which it would pay off the 'capital funding' and 'interest arrears' certificates in date order. It was contemplated that the certificates would be transferable and quoted on the Stock Exchange.

Equity shares of a small nominal value would be issued which would carry no dividend entitlement until all certificates had been paid off.

The Company was advised that this scheme was not 'equitable as between the holders of the several classes of the new securities' as required by the Act[3] and that to promulgate it might render directors open to a civil action by a security holder alleging that he was disadvantaged in comparison with others. Postponement of maturity and reduction in interest rates on all securities by similar fixed amounts as proposed failed to allow for the differential effect on the various classes, as Barings' method of allocation did. Moreover, in the event of a further insolvency the holders of later maturing securities would lose out as compared with those whose certificates had already been paid off. The administrative problems of registering and dealing in what was likely to develop into an extensive range of certificates, many of them for trivial amounts, seemed formidable. Lastly, so long as the surplus fund had to be maintained, the Company's management would be severely hampered, for example as regards their ability to raise funds for capital expenditure or to adjust depreciation as circumstances might require. In general it was felt that the Security Holders Committee's proposal failed to acknowledge that capital had been lost and not merely, as it was said, 'temporarily mislaid'.

Consideration was given to a number of compromises as between the scheme as originally devised, and the Security Holders Committee's and the Company's original concept was modified so as to include the issue of redeemable preference shares, though only to the nominal value of £20 million, far short of any likely write-down.

At the beginning of 1973 the Company was still struggling to assimilate the cargo-handling operations inherited from Smith Coggins and negotiating for the acquisition of the businesses of Port of Liverpool Stevedoring Company and Ocean Port Services, and still subject to Government restraint on raising its charges which, it was estimated, was costing the Company £160,000 per month. The feeling was beginning to intensify that the scheme that the Company was going to have to propose would be so severe that the security holders would be bound to reject it and its effective date would therefore be delayed until 1974, due to the need to have it settled by the High Court. In February the Chairman, at the request of the 'B' directors, wrote to the Minister asking whether the Government would be prepared to give assistance to the Company to enable it to mitigate the severity of the scheme. This request from the 'B' directors had been prompted to some extent by the publication of a Government White Paper on aid to private industry[4] which was reported by *The Times* of 22nd December 1972 under the headline 'D.T.I. officially drops "lame duck" policy in reply to M.P.s' criticism'. As had been expected from soundings already made, the Minister turned down this request.

The first draft of the scheme document was considered by the Finance Committee in mid-March and the fourth draft by the full Board at the beginning of April, when projections prepared by Barings to show the effect on the Company's viability of varying degrees of write-down from 70% to 80% and varied lengths of deferment from three to five years were illustrated. The major features of the scheme, a 70% write-down and four-year postponement, with £20 million nominal of preference shares and £2 million nominal of ordinary shares, were settled at this meeting.

The Company had to exercise the greatest caution in the publication of forecasts to be included in the scheme document in view of the many uncertainties affecting the business. These included, for example, the speed with which the rationalisation of the four merged cargo-handling operations could be achieved, the amount to be received from the Government towards losses on the cargo-handling operations, and the extent to which the Company would be able to increase charges.

Various subsequent drafts of the document were discussed by the directors at meetings in May and formal approval to the final version was given at a meeting on the 21st May. The document was sent to stockholders on the 30th May, in an A4 booklet of 45 densely printed pages. As well as the text of the formal scheme itself, this comprised an explanatory statement of seven pages; an appendix reproducing s.48 of the 1971 Act under which the scheme was made; an appendix of five pages giving revised particulars of the Company's debenture stock; an appendix summarising the principal provisions of the proposed articles of association; an accountant's report on the trading results for 1968–1972 and the balance sheet as at the 31st December 1972; a forecast of trading results for 1973; an appendix listing the Company's debenture stock before and after the scheme and the existing priority borrowing of the Company; a particularly complex appendix of seven pages with two schedules explaining the calculations of entitlements under the scheme; and finally, a page of general information on such topics as directors' interests and material contracts. There was also produced and made available to those who wanted it a ten-page document detailing the calculation of entitlements under the scheme.

In view of the drastic nature of this scheme, the directors conceded explicitly to the stockholders at the beginning of the explanatory statement and again at the end that they were 'under no illusions that it will be welcomed by you'. They declared that it was, nevertheless, what they concluded to be the minimum alteration of the stockholders' rights which would secure (as the Act required), so far as practicable, the financial viability of the Company in light of its current prospects and current and prospective liquid resources 'taking account of future uncertainties'.

The write-down would produce a capital reserve of £64,526,000, of which £21,997,000 was to be applied in issuing shares, £3,955,000 in extinguishing accumulated losses, £20,000,000 to be retained in general reserve to meet future contingencies and the remaining £18,574,000 to be deducted from the book value of the Company's fixed assets, thereby reducing the annual depreciation charge by approximately £670,000.

It was stated that the directors would have liked to have included special provisions to mitigate the scheme's effects on stockholders with small incomes, but were advised that the Act did not permit this.

Though the overall effect of the write-down was approximately 70%, the effect on the nominal value of different stocks varied from 54% to 84%. With a view to improving the potential marketability of the new stocks, it was proposed to reduce the number from 82 to 46.

The preference shares were to be redeemable at the directors' discretion and were to be combined with the ordinary shares which would carry no dividend rights until the preference shares had been redeemed. The reason given for providing that the two types of shares could only be transferred jointly was that if the ordinary shares to which the voting rights were attached were separately transferable, the effective control of the Company could be acquired 'at a very low cost'.

The Secretary of State for the Environment had given authority for the document to state that he would give up priority in respect of his post-November 1970 loans amounting to £21,907,000 if the scheme as proposed, or with such amendments as he approved, was implemented, so that they would rank *pari passu* with the £27,958,000 written-down debenture stock (including some £5 million in respect of his £17 million pre-November 1970 loans).

The new articles of association provided for a board of 11 or 12 directors. Seven 'B' directors were to be elected by the security holders, three 'A' directors to be appointed by the Secretary of State and up to two 'C' directors to be appointed by the other directors after consultation with the trade unions. The Secretary of State's right to appoint 'A' directors was to be secured by a special share to be issued to him, having regard to the Government's considerable financial involvement which, the document said, the Secretary of State expected to continue in the form of grants and loans for the completion of Seaforth. So long as the right to appoint these three 'A' directors existed, the Government were to have no right to vote on the election of 'B' directors.

The explanatory statement concluded in heavy type scored either side by pairs of black lines:

> Your Directors are convinced that a settlement of the prolonged financial crisis of the Port of Liverpool is clearly in the interests of Stockholders. They are of the opinion that the Scheme will re-establish the Company, so far as practicable, as a financially viable entity and will leave the management free to concentrate on the vital task of maximising the efficiency of the Port upon which Stockholders' welfare ultimately depends.
>
> Your Directors therefore recommend most strongly that you vote in favour of the Scheme at the Meetings on 22nd June.

This did not, however, accord with the general reactions to the scheme. *The Times* again devoted a first leader to the affairs of Mersey Docks.

> A SAVAGE WRITE-DOWN
>
> The withholding of Government finance from the Mersey Docks and Harbour Board in November 1970 marked high noon for Selsdon Man.[5] That much is remembered. What is in danger of being forgotten is that relatively little change took place during ensuing months in the Government's policy of industrial disengagement. Although the Government [sic] was forced to withdraw one Bill, a second quickly took its place, turning the board into a public company and calling for the minimum capital

reconstruction necessary to ensure its viability. Despite pressure from the board itself, security holders and others, the Government never showed any inclination to underwrite the holdings of investors who had been long led to regard their stock as effectively Government guaranteed.

So, long after the Government has changed its spots, the Company is having to live in the climate of 1971. Its proposal to write-down the nominal value of its debentures by a savage 70% is a reminder of just how abrasive that climate was. Whether the Company has done what the Act required it to do is a matter for judgement. What is now clear is that the Act itself has wielded a monstrous blow to the small investors whose individual holdings of up to £5000 account for a quarter of the company's stock.

If it is too late for the Government to recant then one must attempt to assess the scheme on its own merits. It is clearly the result of hard and conscientious work by the company and its advisers but is unfortunately open to criticism in several minor points and one major one. Its basic fault which may or may not have been inevitable, is its failure to justify the precise extent of the reconstruction. A highly qualified profit forecast and proforma balance sheet are provided but neither makes it self-evident that so massive a write-down was unavoidable.

At the very least, then, investors have a right to know far more about the assumptions on which the reconstruction was based. They will then be better placed to examine some of the more specific proposals. For instance, the company proposes to issue stockholders with a package of preference and ordinary shares as partial compensation for their loss of security. It could be argued that it has issued too many preference shares (which carry no right to repayment) and should, instead, have written down the debentures by a smaller amount.

It could be argued that no payments to holders of the shares (which are marketable separately from the debentures) should be made while heavy stock redemptions are outstanding; or that the basis on which the debentures were written down paid too much attention to the notional values and not enough to legal rights. These and other matters could be argued out if investors had access to all the information that the company felt able to release.

Investors are being strongly recommended to vote in favour of

> the scheme. To do so would be to indulge in the greatest piece of electoral masochism since the Self-Denying Ordinance.[6] On the other hand, to vote against it would not be a wrecking manoeuvre. The scheme would merely go to the court for approval 'as submitted or with such amendments or additions as the court thinks necessary' to meet the provisions of the Act. In reaching its decision the court could take the advice of professional assessors. The scheme could still be implemented by next year as intended.
>
> A vote against the scheme need on no account be a vote against the company's management who have had a long, distasteful and thankless task to perform in formulating the proposals. It would, however, achieve two objects to which every investor should subscribe. It would allow the arguments for and against the scheme to be debated more fully, without prejudicing the outcome. And it would be a vote of no confidence in the 1971 Mersey Docks and Harbour Act which remains the real villain of the piece.

The Security Holders Committee issued a statement recommending rejection of the scheme in which it strongly urged the Government to take steps to avoid the necessity for a scheme that 'will otherwise impose grievous hardship directly or through institutional funds on many thousands of small investors'.

Mr. Joel Barnett, an Opposition Treasury spokesman, wrote to the Prime Minister likewise urging that the Government should provide money to enable the Company to repay depositors in full.[7] A rare advocate for the scheme was Mr. Philip Chappell, Chairman of the National Ports Council, who expressed his hope that the scheme would be approved 'so that management can get on with the job'.[8]

The meetings of the four classes of stockholders to vote on the scheme were arranged for the afternoon of Friday the 22nd June at the Philharmonic Hall, Liverpool with the A.G.M. to consider the annual report and accounts and to elect directors convened for the morning at the same hall. It was apparent to the directors from the proxy returns received from stockholders before the day of the meetings that the scheme would not get the required approval and that the meetings were likely to be hostile.

The A.G.M. was attended by some 300 stockholders, many of them elderly (the *Financial Times* said it 'looked like a pensioners' treat').[9] The Chairman opened the meeting with a short statement summarising current problems—cargo-handling reorganisation, delay in opening the Seaforth grain terminal and labour shortages—and how the Company was dealing with them, assuring the stockholders of his confidence that given time the efforts to improve the operations and profitability of the port would succeed. He then invited questions from the floor. The session started with a dialogue between the Chairman and Miss Margaret Moston, a 77-year-old retired civil servant who had organised a meeting in Liverpool the previous evening of some of the small stockholders to co-ordinate their opposition to the scheme and to form an action committee to carry on the fight to protect their interests.[10] Her interchange with the Chairman was conducted in a civil manner, but some of the ensuing contributions from the floor were extremely hostile, not to say vituperative. These included proposals that the Company should be wound up, but when the Chairman was pressed to put this formally to the meeting, he had to point out that this could only be done in pursuance of a special resolution and that to do otherwise would be unfair to the many stockholders not present and unaware that such a step was to be proposed. After nearly two hours, the Chairman called for votes on the formal items of business of which notice had been given *viz* the adoption of the report and accounts for 1972, the authorisation for the directors to fix the auditors' remuneration for 1973, and the election of four 'B' directors. On the show of hands on each of these, the resolution was lost but, as the Chairman had told the meeting, he held proxies which enabled him to ensure that they were all carried on a poll by, in round figures, 40 million votes for and 5.8 million votes against the adoption of the report and accounts; 42.6 million for and four million against the authorisation to fix the auditors' fees; and 24.1 million for and 3.7 million against in relation to the election of each 'B' director.

The meetings of the four classes of stockholders were held in the afternoon. At the beginning of the first of these, the meeting of those whose stock derived from the Board's bonds, the Chairman read a prepared statement answering some of the specific criticisms that had been made of the scheme. To counter the criticism that not enough information had been given to justify the proposed severe write-down, he said:

. . . your directors felt that with present and future uncertainties it would be impossible to give forecast figures beyond 1973.

In deciding upon the severity of the capital reconstruction scheme we have been mindful of the need to avoid a further financial crisis, particularly in the early post-scheme years; we have therefore looked to our future profitability providing a degree of interest cover for the fixed-interest bearing debt remaining after the scheme; and making a contribution to the Company's cash flow to enable adequate funds to be available from time to time to meet the postponed redemption on the due dates of the capital debt remaining after the scheme.

The amount proposed to be written off the value of the non-priority borrowings and the proposed period of postponement of maturities have therefore been dictated by the need to provide a minimum interest cover of between one and two times, having regard to the amount anticipated to be available for interest during the early post-scheme years and to ensure that funds will be available during those years to meet the postponed maturities.

If the financial prospects had been better we would have proposed a less severe write-down and an earlier redemption of debenture stock but we felt it necessary to face the facts as they are. Should the future prove that we have been over-pessimistic in regard to the prospective future profitability of the Company, there will be an opportunity for the directors to consider applying profits to the redemption of redeemable preference shares which the scheme proposes shall be issued in recompense in part of capital lost in the write-down of the debenture stock.

To put it very plainly, therefore, this means that the directors cannot foresee the Company having sufficient cash to enable it to do better for security holders than is proposed in the scheme.

Defending the Government's stance, he said: 'it could not be expected that it would be right for the taxpayer to take over the burden of safeguarding the stockholders' interests'. He also referred to the issue of winding-up the Company.

Some of you have suggested, and this was mentioned this morning, that it would be better to close down the docks and share the proceeds out amongst the stockholders. In such a very hypothetical case—because it takes a very prolonged legal process

> that might not be successful anyway—in such a hypothetical case this would not provide you with anything like we now propose based upon the docks as a going concern. The large amounts of money spent on the docks only earn money when operating as part of a port.

He ended his statement by announcing that the proxy votes received were substantially against acceptance of the scheme. This, of course, effectively negated the formal purpose of the meetings. Nevertheless, Mr. Lee, the Public Trustee's representative on the Security Holders Committee, read a short prepared statement of the Committee's criticisms of the scheme. In the Committee's view, the directors had taken a too pessimistic view of the future of the port. They had ignored the effect of inflation which would steadily reduce the cost of servicing the debt. The method of allocation based on relative yields at the time of default was fallacious. The redeemable preference shares were unjustifiable; either the directors should admit they had overestimated the write-down and the preference shares were intended to take up the slack, or, if not, it was misleading to treat it as anything other than equity. The Committee were still advocating the issue of arrears certificates to be given serial priority related to the maturities of the original stocks.

Various other contributions, ranging from denunciations of 'the nefarious House of Commons' and 'Government fraud' to appeals for special treatment for hardship cases ensued before the formal vote was taken. Three hundred and forty two stockholders present are recorded as having voted against approval of the scheme and six for. On the proxy vote 2,089 voted against and 2,325 for; however, each stockholder had one vote for each £1 of stock held and the votes against represented in total £12.8 million as compared with £2.4 million for.

The first meeting lasted about an hour. The second meeting, of the holders of stock deriving from the Board's debentures, started with a similar statement from the Chairman, concluding with a summary of the proxy situation from which it was obvious that this class of stockholder also wanted the scheme to be referred to the High Court. After a rather less angry meeting lasting 40 minutes, the 189 stockholders who voted were unanimously against the scheme and the proxy position was 1,245 stockholders representing £1.5 million for and 1,984 representing £24.5 million against.

The third meeting of the smallest class of stockholders, those holding irredeemable stock, only 17 of whom voted, all against, lasted five minutes. The civil servant who represented the fourth class, the Government, then signified approval in respect of their £19 million holdings of non-priority stock.

In total, of the 33,865 stockholders other than the Government entitled to vote representing £75,493,773, 5,005 representing £43,926,822 voted against the scheme and 3,453 representing £3,954,610 voted for. These results confirmed that the scheme would have to be settled by the High Court.

Chapter 11
IN CHANCERY

The Act required that 'so far as practicable' the High Court should approve the scheme by the 31st December 1973.[1] There was accordingly considerable urgency to prepare the Company's case for submission to the Court and the Company's petition to initiate the proceedings was presented in mid-July, supported by affidavits from the Chairman and the Finance Director setting out the directors' justification for the scheme as presented to the stockholders.

An affidavit from Mr. Peter Baring explained how Barings had prepared schedules of the Company's profitability and liquidity for the years 1973–1992, based on information supplied by the Company, for consideration by the directors when they decided on the scheme; his affidavit also explained the method of calculating entitlements of debenture stock and share capital under the scheme.

On the 30th July 1973 a preliminary hearing to settle the procedure for this novel form of litigation was held before Megarry J. in the unusual setting of Lincolns Inn Hall (which had been decided on as the venue rather than the Royal Courts of Justice because it was thought that a large number of stockholders might attend, though in the event only about 40 were present in person). Megarry J. directed that petitions against the scheme should be lodged by the 30th September and that the hearing should start on the 4th December.

Twenty four petitions were filed, 23 from individual stockholders and one on behalf of the Security Holders Committee. Of the 23 individual petitions, generally from elderly stockholders, 13 were filed through the same firm of local solicitors and were substantially to similar effect, namely that redemption should be deferred 'until the present scheme for reorganisation of the Docks has been completed and it could be shown that the Docks are working profitably so that the Debenture holders may in the near future look forward to redemption of their stock in full. This period would enable the Board

[sic] to realise its substantial assets in land and buildings and so provide it with capital for the purpose of repaying the Debenture Holders'. Another stockholder objected that to be forced to become a shareholder would contravene his religious belief that he should not be 'unequally yoked together with unbelievers (2 Corinthians 6:14)' and his rights under Article 20(2) of the United Nations Universal Declaration of Human Rights. Two others declared that they did not accept that any legislation could alter the terms of bonds issued by the Dock Board. Others suggested that the Court should order immediate repayment of at least part of each debenture and that it should wind up the Company.

The Security Holders Committee criticised the directors' scheme as over-cautious. They attached particular importance to the preservation of debt as against what they described as the 'somewhat bizarre idea of creating redeemable preference stock'. The alternative scheme which they proposed would replace the cancelled debenture stock by unsecured loan stock to the nominal amount of approximately £40 million but repayable at 160p per 100p nominal (i.e. with a 60% premium). This would bear no interest until 1995, but would be repaid out of a loan stock redemption fund into which the Company would be obliged to pay half of its 'surplus income', defined more extensively than profits available for the redemption of preference shares.

In September 1973 seven-figure offers for the South Docks had been received from two property development companies which were substantially in excess of any previous estimates of what the Company and its advisers had expected to receive. It was agreed to give these two parties until the 10th October to put in increased subject-to-contract offers. The higher bid was made by a company called Global Participants (Eire) Limited, as to whose financial standing it proved difficult to get any firm information. After this company had failed to produce the bank guarantee demanded, negotiations were pursued with the Heron Corporation on their offer.

In light of these negotiations which seemed to promise the possibility of obtaining a substantial sum from which the severity of the scheme could be alleviated, application was made to the Court at the end of October to postpone the date of the hearing from December. This application was supported by the Security Holders Committee and the Court put back the start of the hearing until the 19th February

1974. Meanwhile the United Kingdom economy was going through a more than usually troubled period. As a consequence of the Arab-Israeli war of October 1973, the Organisation of Arab Petroleum Exporting Countries had imposed a substantial increase in crude oil prices and a gradually intensifying restriction on supplies to Western countries. This was compounded in this country by a strike of coal miners which led to the imposition by the Government of a State of Emergency and a $3\frac{1}{2}$-day working week. In December the Chancellor of the Exchequer, Mr. Barber, made a statement in Parliament on the economic situation: 'Over the past week or so many have described the situation which we as a nation face as by far the gravest since the end of the war. They do not exaggerate'.[2] (Perhaps a touch of hyperbole, from someone who had lived through the winter of 1947.) His proposals for meeting the crisis included the levying of higher taxes on development and property gains to be detailed in the 1974 Finance Act but to be backdated to the 17th December 1973. This had a dual effect on the Company's hopes of making a sizeable amount from the sale of the South Docks. It was likely to mean a higher tax liability on any receipts, but more immediately it caused Heron to suspend, and in January 1974 to withdraw, its offer.

One small crumb of comfort presented by the Finance Director to the board meeting at the beginning of September was that he had revised his estimate of the loss for 1973 from £4.5 million, as predicted at the time the scheme was devised, to £3 million. The principal causes of this improvement were a less than assumed fall-off in traffic as a result of price increases and increased cargo-handling revenue following the recruitment of dockers. This revision of the forecasts was disclosed in a supplementary affidavit filed by Mr. Wrigglesworth, but it was qualified by the statement that, had the new forecasts been available when the scheme was prepared, it would not have altered the directors' decision. The affidavit also summarised the Company's response to the various petitions filed by the opponents of the Company's scheme.

The economic and energy crises made forecasting especially difficult, and the possibility of a further application for deferment of the Court hearing was considered but quickly rejected on the grounds that there was no certainty when circumstances would improve. By a final irony, on the 7th February 1974, less than a fortnight before the hearing was due to start, the Prime Minister, Mr. Heath, called a

General Election for the 28th February; the Labour Party manifesto published on the 9th February reiterated the commitment to take ports into public ownership.

The hearing opened on the 20th February at the Royal Courts of Justice in London before Templeman J. (who in 1982 became a Lord of Appeal in Ordinary). He was assisted by three assessors—Mr. William Evans, a partner in chartered accountants Tansley Witt, Mr. Angus Murray, an actuary and a former chief investment manager of the Prudential Assurance Company Limited and Mr. Geoffrey (later Lord) Williams, head of the company finance department of J. Schroder Wagg and Company, merchant bankers.

Counsel representing the various parties were: Mr. A. J. Balcombe, Q.C., Mr. Richard Sykes and Miss Mary Arden for the Company; Mr. John Vinelott, Q.C. and Mr. Peter Gibson Q.C., for the Department of the Environment; Mr. Peter Curry, Q.C. and Mr. Oliver Weaver for the Security Holders Committee and some 700 individual stockholders; Mr. Dennis Rice for some 350 individual stockholders; and Mr. H. H. Rajak, on behalf of the Secretary of the Company's staff association, who were concerned to safeguard against any winding-up of the Company, which the judge indicated, early in the proceedings, he was not empowered to do. In addition, Mr. Peter Heath appeared in person. He was a stockbroker, head of a department dealing in Government, local authority, public board and similar securities. Based on this experience, he took a prominent part in the proceedings.

The principal contest was between the Company's and the Security Holders Committee's schemes, but two other schemes were propounded to which the Court gave a courteous hearing. Mr. Rice, representing the views of mainly elderly small stockholders, advocated an indefinite deferment of redemption, with an increase to a market rate of interest on the full nominal value as each issue of debenture stock reached its original maturity date. He endeavoured to show that this should be well within the Company's resources by assuming a very optimistic view of the Company's prospects based on such factors as a favourable sale of the South Docks and a profitable build-up of operations at Seaforth, which the Company's Counsel criticised as 'Alice in Wonderland economics'. The objective of this scheme was to create a security which could either be retained to produce income or sold to produce capital.

Mr. Heath's scheme was diametrically opposite. He proposed that the capital should not be written down, only the interest, which he argued was within the Company's forecast profitability without jeopardising its viability.

The arguments between the Company's scheme and that of the Security Holders Committee focused on two aspects—the difference between conventional preference shares as proposed by the Company and the Committee's more unorthodox form of unsecured loan stock backed by a redemption fund, and whether the Company's prospects justified the severity of a 70% write-down.

The Company introduced evidence from Mr. Charles Ball, an executive director of Kleinwort Benson Ltd., merchant bankers, with knowledge of the ports industry through his part-time membership of the nationalised British Transport Docks Board, operators of Southampton, Hull and other British ports. He testified that any move towards the Committee's proposals was likely to threaten the financial viability of the Company, which the Act enjoined the Court to secure, 'as far as practicable'. His view, which of course was challenged in cross-examination, was that the issue of loan stock ranking alongside unsecured creditors would reduce the Company's credit-worthiness, and the existence of a redemption fund into which the directors were obliged to make prescribed payments would diminish their scope to build up reserves and deter potential lenders of capital.

Mr. John Sanderson, an Under-Secretary in the Ports Directorate of the Department of the Environment, whose affidavits enunciated the Government's view on the rival schemes, warned that any scheme which provided for the issue of 'a substantial amount' of loan stock or 'an excessive amount' of redeemable preference shares might cause the Government to insist on restrictions on the annual rate of redemption as a condition of making further loans to the Company, and to impose strict controls over disposals of capital assets and capital spending. The position with regard to surrender of priority of the post-November 1971 loans, totalling over £23 million by the date of the hearing, was expressly reserved if the directors' scheme should be varied. Counsel for the Department was also at pains to counter any suggestion that the Government could be relied on to step in to save the Company if its viability was threatened in future, as seemed to be implicit in some of the submissions made by the directors' scheme's opponents.

The case for the loan stock was summarised by Mr. J. W. Mulville, Secretary of the Security Holders Committee, under cross-examination by the Company's counsel.

> We felt the great advantage of having loan stock was, first of all, it does enjoy a better ranking in the market because it is an obligation and a debt, it continued the creditor status of the original stockholders and did not convert them into shareholders—which is something in principle we strongly resent—and it also had, we thought, the unique advantage in that it obliged the directors to pay half the profits from time to time towards the redemption of the stock, and that the very existence of that obligation might on occasion enable them to resist pressures, which they would be wholly subject to if their right to redeem the preference shares was merely at their discretion[3] (a reference to potential pressure from the Government as, in effect, the Company's sole bankers).

It became clear that the judge was leaning towards imposing some requirement on the directors to redeem whatever securities were included in the scheme by way of compensation for the write-down. In his final speech, therefore, Mr. Balcombe for the Company indicated a willingness to establish a redemption fund allied to preference shares, though more restricted as to what should be credited to it than the Committee's.

The issue of the size of the write-down turned on the credibility of the Company's financial forecasts and the conclusions to be drawn from them. The directors' original judgement had been based on projections made at the beginning of 1973. After the Finance Director's reassessment of the likely out-turn for 1973 in the autumn of that year, new projections were produced. These took the form of a detailed computer print-out analysing expected profit and cash flow, depreciation, interest, taxation, asset sales and capital expenditure, all analysed into some 60 components. These the Company put forward as a forecast in respect of the years 1973–1978 but thereafter, though extrapolated to 1992, they were described only as 'a framework' to illustrate the long-term effect of the write-down in relation to the few certain factors that could be predicted so far ahead, such as redemptions and interest. In the statement of assumptions underlying these projections, operating expenditure was forecast to rise at 6% against a 5% increase in revenue, on the basis that the Company would not be able to pass on to customers the full effect of cost increases. This, however, was strongly criticised by the Committee—'so untenable as to be absurd' according to Mr. Mulville's affidavit, and 'nonsense' in the words of their Counsel, Mr. Curry. Both Mr. Page and Mr. Wrigglesworth agreed under cross-examination that in practice the directors would never allow this to happen, since it would inevitably at some point lead again to the Company's insolvency.

As the hearing progressed, attention began increasingly to focus on the profit and cash flow projections and, under pressure from the judge, the Company, albeit reluctantly, produced further print-outs to illustrate what would happen if a less pessimistic assumption was made as to the longer-term discrepancy between income and expenditure. The original print-out and the revised version originally produced to the Court were eventually supplemented by another sixteen, based on various assumptions as to net income and level of write-down. As the judge commented, these 'were dragged out of [the Company] like a tooth without anaesthetic'[4] because of their reluctance to see undue reliance placed on the figures after 1978.

The judge and, to a lesser extent, the assessors intervened during the cross-examination of witnesses and subsequently when Counsel and Mr. Heath were summing up their various positions, to probe the answers and submissions. An example of Templeman J.'s trenchant style occurred in an intervention during Mr. Heath's cross-examination of Mr. Wrigglesworth:

> I have got to make you viable. I don't see I'm going to dress you up so that you can walk into Threadneedle Street in 1990. I should not have thought I have got to make you viable longer than it is necessary to pay off the debts which I have now got. I am not here to give you viability in perpetuity.
>
> The foreseeable future, I would have thought, would be when you have paid off the Crown, you have got to pay some of them 100%, and when you have paid off whatever we have to write down off these gentlemen. If I can do that then, so far as I am concerned it is Nunc Dimittis. If, at the end of that, you are still not in a position to put your cap on and go into the banks and ask for money, that is a matter for you.
>
> You will always be in this position: you have got some docks and everybody will want the docks to continue to be operated.

> That is always a powerful factor. But I am not going to give you an extra polish so that you can look big in the City. I know we would all like that, but that is not what I think is viability, as at present advised.[5]

A later interchange with the Government Counsel cut through the niceties.

> *Mr. Vinelott* (after the judge had referred to the Government bringing in the 1971 Act) Which Act is your Lordship referring to?
> *Templeman J.* The 1971 Act that I am wrestling with.
> *Mr. Vinelott* Yes. It of course is technically the Company, my Lord, which proposed that legislation.
> *Templeman J.* It is Parliament that passes it, and we all know when Parliament passes it and when it does not. It is passed if the Government approve of it and it is thrown out if the Government does not. Are not those the facts of life? It may be they have no choice.
> *Mr. Vinelott* My Lord, there are certain very broad qualifications.
> *Templeman J.* Well, you are a 19th Century Whig, perhaps.
> *Mr. Vinelott* There is a distinction, which of course is a very important one, between Parliament and the Government.
> *Templeman J.* Yes, of course.[6]

The evidence finished at lunch time on Wednesday the 27th February, the seventh day of the hearing. Mr. Rice made his final submissions, followed by Mr. Heath. The next day (General Election day) Mr. Wrigglesworth was recalled to produce and be re-examined on four more computer print-out projections that the judge had asked for. Mr. Heath then completed his case and during the rest of that day and the next day Messrs. Curry, Vinelott and Balcombe made their speeches, frequently punctuated by questions from the judge and, less frequently, from the assessors. Judgement was given on Wednesday the 6th March, only five days, including a weekend, later.

The judgement reviewed the history of the financial crisis of the Board/Company from the mid-1950s and then referred to the hardship inflicted on many stockholders as described in affidavits filed in the action: 'Some lenders have made it clear that they expect this Court to do justice by ordering the Company to repay, irrespective of its ability to do so. Those lenders are doomed to be disappointed. I do not complain of their indignation, present and future'.[7]

Of the argument that if the Company was ordered to manage its affairs so as to pay off the debenture stock as soon as possible, efficient management and ruthless increases in port rates would enable payment in full, the judge concluded that the events of the past, the existing burden of debt and future prospects combined to prove that it could not service its existing loan capital and interest.

The judge rejected the scheme suggested by Mr. Rice, on the basis that to convert redeemable securities into irredeemable securities would be a fundamental change that many stockholders would not welcome and this would not, as required by the Act, be equitable as between different classes of stockholders.

In determining 'the amount of money which can safely be extracted from the Company for the benefit of non-priority lenders'[8] he had to take account of the need of the Company to raise fresh loans in the future, but there could be no question of building up the Company's reserves until it could attract fresh loans from the public. The forecasts produced by the Company for the period till the end of 1978, which he accepted as 'properly prudent and cautious',[9] gave, on the basis of a 70% write-down, a cash surplus of over £10 million carried forward from 1974 onwards, which appeared to be 'a comfort rather than a necessity'.[10] In the judgement of Templeman J., a cash reserve of £5 million was sufficient which, from the forecasts produced at his request, was achievable by a 60% write-down. This would have the effect of increasing the amount of debenture stock in the Company's balance sheet from £27 million to £37 million, thus acknowledging that £35.5 million of the original £93.5 million must be regarded as lost, except for any value that might reside in the other securities to be issued under the scheme. He endorsed the four-year deferment of redemption.

On the choice between redeemable preference shares and unsecured loan stock, he unhesitatingly chose loan stock: 'It is important, in my judgement, that there should be presented to the directors of the Company every year a challenge to increase revenue and profits and to pay back to the non-priority lenders as much as possible of the money which was borrowed by the Board and is now owed by the Company'.[11]

He rejected the protests of the Company, supported by the Government, that any obligation attached to the loan stock to make payments would threaten the Company's viability, cause difficulties with trade creditors and contractors and prejudice its ability to raise fresh loans from the Government and elsewhere as 'too shrill'.[12] He prescribed the setting up of a redemption fund into which was to be paid at the end of the year the revenue surplus in excess of £250,000, provided the cash surplus carried forward exceeded £5 million and provided that no more than £1 million should be paid in any year unless the directors so determined. He offered in his judgement to include a power of veto on such payments exercisable by the Government-appointed directors, if they believed such payments could not safely be made. There were also to be paid into this loan stock redemption fund the net proceeds of sale of any surplus assets to the extent that these proceeds were not needed to replace those assets. The £20 million of loan stock, which in the event of liquidation of the Company was to be subordinated to all other creditors, was to carry no interest until 1995 and thereafter (as an incentive to the directors to repay it) any amount outstanding was to bear interest at 10%. The loan stock was to be coupled with £2 million ordinary shares, as in the original scheme.

In order to keep the stockholders in touch with developments, he commended the idea that the directors should 'consider recommendations and criticisms offered by experienced representatives of the lenders'.

To translate this judgement into a scheme, the Act effectively imposed a three-week timescale.[13] This involved a recalculation of the entitlements of the various classes of stockholders in accordance with what had come to be called 'the Baring formula', as to which the judge had told Mr. Baring 'There has been a chorus of universal approval of the very complicated way you worked it out and as far as I can see not the slightest criticism of how it does work out'.[14] This necessitated the calculation of a separate schedule of the entitlements of those who had received part redemption under the small income relief provision of the Act, amounting in all to more than £350,000, covering more than 1,500 applicants. The revised balance sheet showed assets written down by some £18.5 million, thereby reducing the annual depreciation charge by about £770,000. The balance of the difference between the original stock and the aggregate nominal value of the new securities was applied in writing off accumulated losses and creating an £8.3 million general reserve.

The veto on redemption from annual profits offered by the judge was amended to provide that the Secretary of State (rather than the Government-appointed directors) could delay (rather than veto) the redemption if he was of the opinion that such payment might jeopardise the Company's financial viability; the amount not paid in any year was to be carried forward to the next year.

Provisions were included in the terms of the loan stock for the appointment of an Advisory Committee of three members, to be elected by the loan stock holders to make recommendations to the directors and to report on the affairs of the Company.

The formal scheme incorporating these and other detailed terms was approved by the judge and came into effect on the 27th March 1974, three years and three months after the Board had defaulted on its January 1971 bond redemption.

Chapter 12
EPILOGUE

The effect of the Scheme on the Company's finances was described in the document sent to stockholders in May 1974. The debenture stock was written down from approximately £92,407,000 to approximately £37,110,000. After the issue of approximately £22,018,700 in nominal value of loan stock and ordinary shares, a capital reserve of approximately £33,278,300 was created. Out of this reserve, the directors applied £18,574,000 in writing down the book value of the Company's fixed assets and £6,396,000 in extinguishing accumulated losses, retaining £8,308,300 in a general reserve to meet future contingencies.

The write-down of the fixed assets resulted in a reduction in the annual depreciation charge of approximately £770,000 in 1974, with a consequential effect on the reported results. The full year reduction in the Company's interest payments as shown in the pro-forma accounts for 1973 would have fallen from £5,923,000 to £4,060,000 (inc. £1,864,000 payable to the Government on their part of its debt which was not affected by the scheme) had the scheme been effective in 1973; the actual figure was reduced by 30% under the terms of the 1971 Act. In fact, the reduction in the interest charge in the reported accounts for 1975, the first full year in which the scheme was effective, was £1,474,000 down on 1973's, and depreciation down by £200,000, but the loss for 1975 was £8,089,000 as against losses of £2,506,000 in 1973 and £965,000 in 1974.

The Scheme did not therefore immediately transform the Company's fortunes. On the contrary, its travails continued for several years, as can be traced through subsequent annual reports and accounts and Chairmen's statements. Nationalisation of the ports, promised by the Labour party in its 1974 election manifesto, never in fact took place, presumably because the Labour Government decided it had too small a majority throughout the period to 1979 when it was in office to get such a controversial policy through Parliament. Table 2

Table 2 *Main operating statistics of the Mersey Docks and Harbour Company, 1973–1988*

Year	Cargo tonnage (thousand tons)	Number of vessels using Company facilities	N.R.T. of vessels (1,000t)	Number of employees (year average)	Turnover (£ thousand)	Operating profit (loss) (£ thousand)	Interest paid (£ thousand)	Overall profit (loss) (£ thousand)
1973	25,895	6,397	20,081	9,485	37,233	4,561	5,350	(2,506)
1974	26,384	5,618	20,250	9,626	39,758	2,958	4,011	(965)
1975	22,450	5,526	19,082	9,410	52,171	7,185	3,876	(8,089)
1976	21,269	5,438	G.R.T. (1,000T) 32,576	8,529	60,767	12,506	4,249	4,045
1977	18,471	5,369	31,883	8,275	62,661	12,213	4,165	4,106
1978	15,919	5,439	29,341	8,094	64,715	9,332	4,420	(11,470)
1979	15,375	5,366	29,414	7,397	66,943	6,385	4,793	(7,462)
1980	12,477	4,540	26,372	6,481	65,644	5,025	5,499	(6,250)
1981	11,042	3,831	23,432	5,647	61,635	1,250	5,417	5,062
1982	9,300	3,484	20,368	4,281	55,544	(2,337)	4,131	6,586
1983	10,671	3,504	21,457	3,297	56,990	6,790	880	6,554
1984	9,181	3,419	19,052	3,001	50,234	1,921	1,114	(343)
1985				2,870	52,961	3,241	837	2,004
1986				2,571	51,393	3,172	1,094	1,328
1987	(10,200)			2,440	53,935	5,034	1,279	3,755
1988	(19,500)			2,281	55,159	6,700	895	5,865

Notes: N.R.T. = net registered tonnage; G.R.T. = gross registered tonnage. No statistics of cargo tonnage and volume of shipping were given in the Company's 1985–1988 Reports. The 1987 and 1988 cargo tonnages are taken from the Chairman's 1988 statement.

summarises some of the main statistics which illustrate the Company's progress from 1973 to 1988.

Behind these bare statistics lie herculean efforts by the Company's management to revive its fortunes in the face of such difficulties as exceptionally turbulent labour relations (resulting especially from the radical reshaping of the Port), adverse trade trends and an unfavourable local property market. The most consistent feature of the period was the unremitting reduction in the number of Company employees, from 9,626 in 1974 to 2,281 in 1988. This reduction was necessitated to a large extent by the decline in work for registered dock workers resulting partly from fluctuations in trade levels, but in the longer term from changes in cargo-handling methods. The surplus of dockers led to the payment by the Company of large sums in fall-back pay, e.g. £2 million in 1975, £1.7 million in 1976, £1.4 million in 1977 and £1.8 million in 1978. The Company's problems were compounded by the requirement under the Aldington-Jones report to absorb most of the registered dock workers made redundant by private firms in the Port who went out of business over these years.

To assist in tackling the persistent problem of surplus dock labour, in other ports as well as Liverpool, the Government, under pressure from port authorities, helped fund voluntary severance schemes. A major scheme proposed by the Company in 1986 was delayed for a year by E.E.C. queries as to whether Government contributions contravened European competition policies. When the Dock Labour Scheme was finally abolished in 1989 the resultant strike is estimated to have cost the Company £3.4 million. In 1990 the Company withdrew from cargo-handling operations for general cargo at a cost of £4.3 million; the Port thus reverted to the pre-1966 system whereby all such cargo-handling operations were carried out by private firms, though the Company held an interest in some of these firms.

Meanwhile, the focus of the Company's business was changing. Seaforth became increasingly the principal centre of the Company's dock operations, with modern facilities for handling containers, timber and grain (both import and export) in bulk. The closed South Docks were transferred by Government Order to the newly established Merseyside Development Corporation[1] in 1981 and in March 1987 the Lands Tribunal decided that the compensation due to the Company for this expropriation was just over £3 million, disappointingly less than the Company had expected.

Meanwhile, many changes were taking place in the Company's traditional operations. For example, the closure of Tate & Lyle's Liverpool refinery in the late 1970s brought to an end a long-standing import traffic through the Port. The tobacco warehousing operation which had been an important part of the Port's business for 200 years was closed in 1980. The towing away of Princes Landing Stage in 1977 symbolised the demise of the Port's passenger liner trade.

Though the Company's business remained predominantly that of a traditional dock and harbour authority, it also exploited new opportunities. A consultancy department secured contracts in Saudi Arabia in 1975 and subsequently worldwide. In November 1984 the Company opened the United Kingdom's first and still its largest Freeport, covering 600 acres of dock estate from Langton Dock to Seaforth, surrounded by 3km of steel palisade fencing.

By 1988 the Company was beginning to establish a record of profitability. Only 32p had been paid off the unsecured loan stock,[2] almost entirely from the proceeds of land sales. It was considered by the directors that it would in the immediate future be more advantageous to the Company to participate in the development of any surplus land rather than to sell it, a policy which would of course limit future redemptions.

However, the date when it would have to start paying interest on any amount outstanding, January 1995, was approaching. It was revealed, accordingly, in the preliminary announcement of the results for 1988 (a profit of £5.9 million, an increase of 56% on the previous year) that the Company was in negotiation with the Government on a possible capital reorganisation. The resultant agreement was announced on the 2nd May 1989 and details of the proposed capital reorganisation were circulated to holders of the combined units on the 4th May.

In essence the scheme was for the capitalisation of the loan stock into ordinary shares in the ratio of three 10p nominal ordinary shares for one combined unit (comprising a 10p ordinary share and 68p nominal of loan stock). For its part the Government had agreed to waive the repayment of grants totalling £110 million and the cancellation of £1.5 million loans which had been made under the Ports (Financial Assistance) Act 1981, principally to finance severance payments to redundant employees. This was in addition to £30 million written off the Company's debt to the Government in 1983. As against this, the Company's accumulated tax losses of approximately £109 million were reduced by approximately £99.5 million. These proposals were put to an extraordinary general meeting on 30th May and approved by holders of the combined units (including the Government's $22\frac{2}{3}$% holding).

The 1989 capital reorganisation completed the transformation of the Mersey Docks and Harbour Board, initiated by the Mersey Docks and Harbour Act 1971, into as nearly normal a public limited liability company as possible, having regard to the fact that it remains under a statutory duty to maintain, operate and improve the Port of Liverpool of which it could be relieved only by an Act of Parliament.

The cost of the transformation from Board to Company initially fell largely on the 25,500 holders of the £75.75 million non-priority debt, by virtue first of the moratorium on repayment and 30% reduction in interest in the period 1971–74, and then of the 1974 capital write-down. Of this debt, £9 million was held by some 18,500 holders of bonds and other securities of £1,000 or less, with an average holding of £500.

However, the 1974 capital reconstruction allotted to those who had suffered in this way a unique form of equity, combined units of unsecured loan stock and ordinary shares, so that they might share the benefit of any upturn in the Company's fortunes. On the eve of the opening of dealings in the written-down debentures and the combined units at the end of May 1974, the Financial Editor of *The Times* wrote in his column[3] that

> . . . the temptation for holders to cut their losses and forget the whole, unhappy episode must be strong. Many holders, particularly elderly ones, may have no personal option but to realise what hard cash they can. The new debentures will doubtless trade at a discount on blue-chip debentures, given their woeful antecedence and the pent-up selling pressures.

After weighing-up the pros and cons of selling debentures, including the possibility of nationalisation undoing the effect of the 1971 Act, his column continued

> However, the problems in assessing the debentures are as nothing compared to the problems of evaluating the new stock/share units. For the real irony of the situation is that investors who

> originally turned to the old Board for near gilt-edged security now find themselves holding the most potentially volatile paper ever to receive a Stock Exchange quote.

He then assessed the prospects for redemption of the unsecured loan stock under the High Court formula and continued

> Given that the Company's entire land and buildings are valued at only £23 million and that the pitfalls on the road for profitability are still considerable, the realistic range of expectations for the new units is more limited.
>
> But it is still wide enough to suggest that holders would be ill-advised to sell if, as expected, the units start their life this week on a penny-stock basis. Their faith has been sorely tested in the past, but patience could now be rewarded.

On the opening of dealings on 28th May, the Company's debentures were indeed heavily discounted.[4] For example, the $3\frac{1}{4}$% 1974/84 stock started at £18.50 for £100 nominal and drifted down during the day to £13.50. As for the combined units, the Stock Exchange indicated its assessment of the Company's prospects by quoting the shares at 2p(buy) and 4p(sell) and it was indeed some years before the Company's fortunes recovered sufficiently to give these combined units any substantial value. Eventually, however, those who retained them, either through acumen or inertia (and even more those who purchased them as a speculation), began to reap the benefit.[5]

This may be illustrated by the case of a holder of an 8% Dock Board bond originally due for redemption on the 1st January 1971. There were some 860 holders of such bonds, with an aggregate value in excess of £6 million; of this just over £300,000 was held by 724 holders of £1,000 or less. A holder of a £1,000 bond would have had redemption deferred until the 1st January 1975 and reduced to £397.80. In the moratorium period he would have received interest to the value of £213.40. In addition, he would have been allotted 278 combined units. Had he retained these units he would have received £88.90 by way of redemption payments under the terms of the loan stock. In the period up to the 1989 capital reorganisation, the price of these combined units reached 700p each, i.e. £1,946 for our hypothetical bondholder. Since the allotment of three shares for each combined unit in 1989 the share price has risen as high as 534p, at which the bondholder's shares would have been worth £4,454. In the three years 1990 to 1993 he would have received £126.43 (gross) in dividends. Furthermore, when the Company made a rights issue in 1993 he could have sold his rights for £677. This could be summarised as follows:

Moratorium interest	213
Jan. 1975 redemption	398
Loan stock redemption	89
Value of post 1989 shares	4454
Dividends 1990–93	126
Sale of rights	667
	5947

This is, of course, a very crude calculation. First, it assumes an investor who sells out at the top of the market and it ignores dealing expenses. Above all, it takes no account of the effects of inflation. Nevertheless, it shows that some at least of the losses suffered more than 20 years previously were more than recouped.

NOTES AND SOURCES

Though most of the pre-1970 records of The Mersey Docks and Harbour Board are now held in the archives of the National Museums and Galleries on Merseyside at the Liverpool Maritime Museum, Albert Dock, the records relating to the financial crisis are still retained by the Company. The Company have allowed me full access to these records, principally board and committee minutes; I have tried to make clear in the text the provenance of my information. I have also had access to the transcripts of the hearings (which were, of course, public) before the House of Commons Select Committee and the High Court.

For the chapters relating to the Board's finances before 1970 I have relied extensively on an unpublished paper written by the late Mr. S. H. Green in 1971 shortly after his retirement as Secretary of the Board, with assistance from Messrs. C. H. Campbell, A. P. Nute and the present author.

Until 1970 the Secretariat of the Board used to produce a summary of all decisions of the board and committees under a wide variety of discrete headings. These worked-up papers (W.U.P.s), now deposited with the Museum archives, are an invaluable source of information, much of it going right back to the incorporation of the Board. For example, W.U.P.S.53 traces the history of the Board's sinking funds.

The best general history of the Board up to 1963 is *Western Gateway* by the late Mr. A. S. Mountfield, General Manager and Secretary from 1957 to 1962.

Chapter 1: The Public Trust

1. A test case brought by merchants Bolton, Ogden and Co. against the Corporation in 1833 had established the legality of such application of the Town Dues, but the resentment persisted.
2. Mersey Conservancy Act 1842.
3. Ministry of Transport Act 1919.

4. S.1 1965 No. 1503.
5. Sir Joseph Cleary (1902–1993) had a long and distinguished career as a Labour politician, mainly in local government. In 1935 he was M.P. for the Wavertree division of Liverpool for eight months, having been elected at a by-election where the Conservative vote was split by Randolph Churchill's standing as an Independent Conservative. The by-election is described in the paper 'A Mad Hatter contest from beginning to end' by David Dutton in the *Transactions of the Historic Society of Lancashire and Cheshire* for 1993, Vol. 142, p. 179.
6. Liverpool University Press, 1965.
7. The Board was empowered to issue irredeemable annuities by The Mersey Dock Acts Consolidation Act 1858 ss.287–296.
8. The history of the Sinking Fund is recorded in W.U.P.S.53. In 1970 the Board paid in £1,159,338. Payments into the Fund came mainly from revenue, supplemented occasionally by receipts from capital sales. The Fund was applied chiefly to refund bond redemptions.

Chapter 2: Political Background

1. 1962, Command 1824.
2. Rochdale Report, para.177.
3. Ibid., para.93.
4. Ibid., para.591.
5. Ibid., para.598/9.
6. Ibid., para.555.
7. Ibid., para.554.
8. Ibid., para.560.
9. Ibid., para.261.
10. Ibid., para.660.
11. Harbours Act 1964, s.9.
12. Ibid., s.1 and s.9(6).
13. Control of Harbour Development Order 1964, S.1.1964 No. 1386.
14. Control of Harbour (Amendment) Development Order 1971. S.1.1971 No. 1874.
15. Established by the Dock Workers (Regulation of Employment) Order S R and O 1947 No. 1189 made under the Dock Workers (Regulation of Employment) Act 1946.

16. *Unofficial Stoppages in the London Docks*, 1957, Cmd. 8236.
17. *Inquiry into the Operation of the Dock Labour Scheme*, 1956, Cmd.9813.
18. *Report into Wages Dispute of N.J.C.*, 1964, Cmd. 2523; *Report into Decasualisation and Causes of Dissension*, 1965, Cmd. 2734; *Report into Wages Structure and Level of Pay*, 1966, Cmd. 3104.
19. *Report into Locally Determined Aspects of Payment in Liverpool*, 1967.
20. *Report into Wage Dispute of N.J.C. for the Port Transport Industry*, 1970, Cmd. 4429.
21. The bibliography to *Dockers* by David F. Wilson (1972, Fontana) lists 32 reports of inquiries into dock labour problems between 1945 and 1970.
22. Rochdale Report Chapter 27.
23. Devlin Report 1965, *Plan of Action*, pp. 125–29.
24. Hansard (H.C.) 30.10.68 Col. 33.
25. *Reorganisation of the Ports*, Cmd.3903.
26. Nationalised bodies of which he was a member were the British Steel Corporation 1967–70, British Airways Board 1971–1981 and British Rail Board, Chairman 1976–83.
27. Hansard (H.C.) 29.4.70 Col. 1269. Mr. Heseltine was the Parliamentary Secretary to the Minister of Transport from June to October 1970 and Parliamentary Under Secretary of State, Department of Environment, from 1970 to 1972.

Chapter 3: 1965–1970

1. Mersey Docks and Harbour Board Revision Order 1965, S.1. 1903.
2. Seaforth was initially conceived of as a dock for conventional general cargo ships, with a finger layout of 12/14 berths and two bulk-cargo berths. Fortunately, the implications of the container revolution were realised in time for the layout to be changed to its present configuration.
3. Working documents intended as a basis for discussion, published 6th July 1967. *The Times*, 7th July 1967.
4. Inquiry by Mr. D. Steele F.C.A., November 1966.
5. I hope I will not be thought to be doubting my readers' classical education if I remind them that Cassandra was a prophetess whose predictions were always correct. However, they were

never believed, because she had been cursed for repulsing the advances of Apollo (where the analogy with Barings breaks down).

6. Devlin Report, 1965, Cmd. 2734, paras. 287/8.

Chapter 4: The Crisis Breaks

1. Hansard (H.C.) 11.11.70 col. 398 et seq.
2. According to *The Times* of the 12th November 1970, 'The reading of the statement was punctuated by shocked exclamations from the Opposition side and then by bursts of laughter when Mr. Corfield entered the political minefield of the Industrial Reorganisation Corporation [set up by the previous Labour Government] on which the Government has previously pronounced sentence of death'.
3. Rolls-Royce (Purchase) Act 1971.
4. *The Times*, 21st November 1970.
5. *The Times*, 28th November 1970.

Chapter 5: The End of the Beginning

1. *Spycatcher*, 1987 (William Heinemann, Australia) p. 31: 'Before finally joining A2 as a Scientific Officer I underwent 2 days training. The Training programme was the responsibility of a tough, no-nonsense officer named John Cuckney. We got on well . . . Cuckney was his own man and had broad horizons beyond the office. It was no surprise to me when he left MI5 to pursue a successful career in business'. A résumé of Sir John Cuckney's career was given in a Profile on him in *The Independent* newspaper on the 19th March 1994.
2. Hansard (H.C.) 30.11.70 Col. 903.
3. Ibid., Col. 907.
4. Ibid., Col. 1083 et seq.
5. Ibid., Col. 1095.
6. Ibid., Col. 911.
7. Hansard (H.C.) 1.12.70 Col. 1096.
8. Ibid.
9. Ibid., Col. 1097 et seq.
10. Ibid., Col. 1105.
11. Ibid., Col. 1146.

12. Hansard (H.C.) 18.12.70 Col. 1733 et seq.
13. Ibid., Col. 1741.

Chapter 6: The Executive Committee

1. Mersey Dock Acts Consolidation Act 1858, Sch.F.
2. Circular to 'holders of the Capital Debt', 29th January 1971.
3. *The Times*, 30th January 1971, quoted by Financial Editor.
4. February 1971, No. 25.
5. London *Evening Standard*, 17th March 1971.
6. Erskine May, *Parliamentary Practice*, 18th Edition (1971), pp. 817–18.
7. Hansard (H.C.) 27.4.71 Col. 324.
8. Ibid., Col. 364.
9. Ibid., Col. 340.
10. Ibid., Col. 351.
11. Ibid., Col. 352.
12. Ibid., Col. 356.

Chapter 7: In Committee

1. Miss Mary Arden, just called to the Bar, held a noting brief for the Board. She subsequently had a distinguished career at the Chancery Bar, culminating in her appointment as a High Court Judge, Chancery Division, in 1993.
2. Transcript of Committee proceedings, Day 3, p.2.
3. Ibid., Day 5, pp. 44–45 and 53–54.
4. Ibid., Day 5, p. 48.
5. Ibid., Day 5, p. 56.
6. Ibid., Day 5, p. 67.
7. Ibid., Day 5, p. 36.
8. Ibid., Day 5, p. 96.
9. Ibid., Day 3, p. 21.
10. Ibid., Day 7, p. 19 et seq.
11. Ibid., Day 7, p. 30.
12. Ibid., Day 7, p. 32–33.
13. Ibid., Day 7, p. 42.
14. Ibid., Day 7, p. 44.
15. Ibid., Day 7, p. 46.
16. Ibid., Day 7, p. 47.
17. Ibid., Day 7, p. 47.

18. Ibid., Day 8, p. 33 et seq.
19. Ibid., Day 9, p.1.
20. Hansard (H.C.) 21.6.71 Col. 1096.
21. Transcript of Committee proceedings, Day 7, p. 48.
22. Ibid., Day 7, p. 47.
23. Hansard (H.C.) 21.6.71 Col. 1080/2.
24. Ibid., Col. 1114.
25. Hansard (H.C.) 1.7.71 Col. 776/7.
26. Hansard (H.L.) 13.7.71 Col. 207 et seq.

Chapter 8: Business as Usual

1. Hansard (H.C.) 30.7.71 written answers Col. 198.
2. *Liverpool Daily Post*, 29th June 1971.
3. *The Daily Telegraph*, 29th June 1971.
4. The official opening of Seaforth was carried out by H.R.H. Princess Anne on the 18th July 1973, when she named it Royal Seaforth Dock.

Chapter 9: Annus Horribilis

1. *Liverpool Daily Post*, 10th April 1972.
2. *Union Jack*, the autobiography of Jack Jones (Collins, 1986) p. 29.
3. Hansard (H.C.) 25.7.72 Col. 1559.
4. *Cargo Handling*, 5th March 1973.
5. Cmd. 5125, subsequently promulgated as the Counter-Inflation (Temporary Provisions) Act 1972 passed on the 30th November 1972, which imposed a 90-day freeze on prices, charges for services, pay, dividends and rents.

Chapter 10: The Scheme: Phase One

1. Died January 1994.
2. Now the Liverpool John Moores University.
3. Mersey Docks and Harbour Act 1971 (S.48(1)(a)).
4. *Public Money in the Private Sector*; Government Observations on the 6th Report of the Expenditure Committee.
5. In January 1960 leading Conservative politicians met at Selsdon Park Hotel to discuss future policy. The Prime Minister, Mr. Harold Wilson, was quoted as saying 'Selsdon Man is designing a system of society for the ruthless and pushing'.

6. In December 1644 (during the Civil War) Parliament passed an Ordinance that 'no Member of either House during the Time of War shall have or execute any Office or Command Military or Civil'.
7. *The Financial Times*, 2nd July 1973.
8. *The Times*, 1st June 1973.
9. *The Financial Times*, 23rd July 1973.
10. *Liverpool Daily Post*, 22nd July 1973.

Chapter 11: In Chancery

1. Mersey Docks and Harbour Act 1971, s.48(4)(c).
2. Hansard (H.C.) 17.12.73 Col. 952.
3. Court transcript, Day 5, p. 43.
4. Ibid., Day 6, p. 3.
5. Ibid., Day 4, p. 47.
6. Ibid., Day 6, p. 26.
7. Judgement transcript, p. 7.
8. Ibid., p. 12.
9. Ibid., p. 17.
10. Ibid., p. 17.
11. Ibid., p. 19.
12. Ibid., p. 19.
13. Mersey Docks and Harbour Act 1971, s.49(1)(b).
14. Court transcript, Day 5 p. 30. See also Judgement transcript, p. 22.

Chapter 12: Epilogue

The material for the summary history of the Company's affairs from 1974 to 1988 is taken mainly from the annual reports and accounts and Chairmen's statements for those years. The Chairmen were:

April 1972–June 1977	Mr. John Page, O.B.E.
June 1977–June 1980	Sir Arthur Peterson, K.C.B., M.V.O.
June 1980–June 1984	Sir John Page, O.B.E.
June 1984–July 1987	Mr. J. B. Fitzpatrick, C.B.E.
August 1987–September 1993	Mr. W. B. Slater, C.B.E., V.R.D.

Chief Executives were:

April 1974–September 1975	Mr. G. W. Brimyard and Mr. J. B. Fitzpatrick (Joint Managing Directors)
September 1975–March 1977	Mr. John Page, O.B.E. (also Chairman)
March 1977–June 1984	Mr. J. B. Fitzpatrick, C.B.E.
June 1984 to date	Mr. P. T. Furlong.

1. Merseyside Development Corporation, established from the 25th March 1981 by the Merseyside Development Corporation (Area and Constitution) Order 1980, S.I., 1981, No. 481.
2. Repayments of loan stock were as follows:

11th August 1975	2p	Proceeds of land sales
13th June 1977	3p	Payment from profits
3rd July 1978	3p	Payment from profits
5th July 1982	2p	Proceeds of land sales
26th September 1983	19p	Advance payment of compensation for South Docks compulsory purchase.
27th May 1985	2p	Proceeds of land sales
6th August 1987	1p	Proceeds of land sales
	32p	Total

3. *The Times*, 7th March 1974.
4. Prices of the Company's securities taken from the *Liverpool Daily Post*, 29th May 1974.
5. After the buying price attained double figures in the autumn of 1977 and reached 35p in the following winter, it fell back to single figures by the summer of 1980. From the following spring it began to climb again, getting as high as 61p in September 1983. The real surge started in June 1987 when the price increased from 80p per unit to 440p by September. The maximum price of 700p was quoted for about two weeks in May 1989. (I am indebted to Mr. F. Dullaghan of the Company for these figures.)

   In compliance with company law, the directors of the Company in their reports published with the Annual Accounts record the identity of holders of 'substantial shareholdings' (5% until 1989; thereafter 3%) and the number of shares held by directors.

The Secretary of State for Transport has always been the major shareholder—20.67% until the 1993 rights issue, 13.91% since. The first reference to a substantial shareholding by any other party was in the 1982 report when Robert Fleming Nominees Limited were recorded as holding 5.34% of the Company's shares. Subsequent reports record several other substantial shareholdings, notably a 10.58% holding by Peel Holdings plc revealed in the 1987 report, acquired to lay the ground for a possible take-over bid for the Company which never took place.

Only two directors have been recorded as having beneficial shareholdings of any significant size. Mr. J. D. Abell was recorded as holding 500,000 shares when he became a 'B' director in April 1981, of which he sold 400,000 in 1983 and the remaining 100,000 in 1985. He bought 166,000 shares in 1987 and resigned from the Board in May 1989. Mr. T. Edwards, a 'B' director from July 1984 to October 1987, held beneficially 200,000 shares.

CHRONOLOGY (TO 1974)

1715:	First dock in Liverpool.
1st January 1858:	Incorporation of Mersey Docks and Harbour Board.
1962:	Rochdale Report.
1964:	Harbours Act.
1964–66:	Devlin Reports on Dock Labour Scheme.
April 1966:	Election of Labour Government. Board starts container-handling operations.
June 1966:	Mersey Docks and Harbour Board (Seaforth Works) Act.
March 1967:	Government consent given to start of Seaforth.
July 1967:	Government consultation paper proposing nationalisation of ports by 1st January 1970.
August 1968:	Treasury and Bank of England refuse Board permission to issue new debenture stock.
October 1968	Board issue £8.5m of 8% bonds for two to five years.
July 1969:	J. C. Taylor succeeds M. D. Oliphant as Chairman of the Board.
November 1969:	Ports Bill introduced into Parliament.
18th June 1970:	Election of Conservative Government.
29th July 1970	J. C. Taylor and R. S. F. Edwards meet Minister of Transport Industries to discuss Board's finances. Binder Hamlyn appointed to advise.
4th September 1970:	Board offers to renew £1 million of bonds and to accept new money.
10th September 1970:	Binder Hamlyn preliminary report on Board's finances.
15th September 1970:	Board withdraws offer to renew bonds and returns money already received.

28th September 1970:	Board issues press notice announcing 'a serious financial situation'. Copy sent to all security holders with copy of letter from Minister.
2nd November 1970:	Board sends outline plan to Minister.
27th November 1970:	Board deposits Private Bill proposing two-year moratorium and 30% write-down of debt.
30th November 1970:	Board meets Minister in London and agrees to appoint J. G. Cuckney as Chairman and to set up Executive Committee. Minister makes statement in Parliament.
1st December 1970:	Emergency debate in House of Commons.
4th December 1970:	High Court appoints Receiver of Rates, on Government application.
1st January 1971:	Board defaults on payment of £6 million of Bonds. Various institutions commence actions to enforce payment.
29th January 1971:	Circular to security holders announcing withdrawal of Bill deposited in November and summarising Board's revised proposals.
13th February 1971:	New Bill deposited.
26th April 1971:	1970 Accounts published and copy sent to all security holders, for first time.
4th May–27th May 1971:	House of Commons Select Committee hearing to consider Board's Bill.
9th June 1971:	Committee's decision on Bill.
27th July 1971	Bill receives Royal Assent.
30th July 1971:	Mersey Docks and Harbour Board meets for last time.
3rd November 1971:	Mersey Docks and Harbour Company's first general meeting.
6th December 1971:	*Tasmania Star* first ship to enter Seaforth.
26th April 1972:	J. J. Page succeeds J. G. Cuckney as Chairman.
5th May 1972:	Aldington-Jones Committee set up to consider 'problems confronting the ports industry'.

21st July 1972:	Five London dockers imprisoned for contempt of National Industrial Relations Court, precipitating strikes at London, Hull and Liverpool.
17th September 1972:	Company takes over A. E. Smith Coggins Limited.
29th September 1972:	South Docks closed.
February 1973:	Company takes over Port of Liverpool Stevedoring Co. Limited and Ocean Port Services Limited.
30th May 1973:	Company's Scheme proposals circularised to stockholders.
22nd June 1973:	A.G.M. and class meetings of stockholders, who reject Company's Scheme proposals.
December 1973:	Government imposes State of Emergency and 3½-day working week.
20th February–28th February 1974:	High Court hearing into Scheme.
28th February 1974:	General Election; Labour Government supplants Conservatives.
6th March 1974:	High Court judgement.
27th March 1974:	Scheme as decreed by Court comes into effect.
(30th May 1989:	Company's shareholders approve Capital Reorganisation.)

INDEX